# Conceptual Blockbusting

Also by James L. Adams
*The Care and Feeding of Ideas: A Guide to Encouraging Creativity*
*Flying Buttresses, Entropy, and O-Rings—The World of an Engineer*

# Conceptual Blockbusting

## A GUIDE TO BETTER IDEAS

*Fourth Edition*

**James L. Adams**

BASIC
BOOKS

A Member of the Perseus Books Group
New York

Many of the designations used by manufacturers and sellers to distinguish their products are claimed as trademarks. Where those designations appear in this book and Basic Books was aware of a trademark claim, the designations have been printed in initial capital letters.

Library of Congress catalog card number is available

Copyright © 1974, 1976, 1979, 1986, 2001 by James L. Adams
Previously published by Perseus Publishing
Published by Basic Books, A Member of the Perseus Books Group

ISBN-13: 978-0-7382-0537-3
ISBN-10: 0-7382-0537-0

Find us on the World Wide Web at http://www.basicbooks.com

Books published by Basic Books are available at special discounts for bulk purchases in the U.S. by corporations, institutions, and other organizations. For more information, please contact the Special Markets Department at the Perseus Books Group, 11 Cambridge Center, Cambridge, MA 02142, or call (617) 252-5298.

Text design by Nighthawk Design
Set in 10.5 point Janson Text by Bookcomp, Inc.

First printing, September 2001
15  14

# CONTENTS

# PREFACE

FEW PEOPLE LIKE PROBLEMS. Hence the natural tendency in problem-solving is to pick the first solution that comes to mind and run with it. The disadvantage of this approach is that you may run either off a cliff or into a worse problem than you started with. A better strategy in solving problems is to select the most attractive path from many ideas, or concepts. This book is concerned with the cultivation of idea-having and problem-solving abilities.

Since I am a teacher of and consultant in engineering and management, the majority of my contacts are with people who are analytical, quantitative, verbal, and logical. These are certainly excellent traits for any problem-solver. However, so is the ability to conceptualize freely, an activity that requires a somewhat broader thinking vocabulary. I am deeply concerned with attempting to better define this vocabulary and with helping people expand in this direction. This book reflects that concern. Although I originally began this quest in an engineering environment, my experience with people in other fields has convinced me that the material in this book is applicable to most walks of life.

You will find little within about how to be more verbal or analytical, although these are both powerful problem-solving tools. Instead the book concentrates upon aspects of thinking that are useful in improving one's conceptual abilities and that I feel are underemphasized in many people's education. Although the book focuses upon conceptualization, these aspects of thinking are also pertinent in other parts of the problem-solving process. Much of the book's emphasis is on creativity, since a good conceptualizer must be a creative conceptualizer. The mental characteristics that seem to make one creative not only are valuable in idea-having, but also better equip one to find and define problems and implement the resulting solutions.

The material herein draws upon a multitude of sources. I was first introduced to thinking about thinking by the late John E. Arnold, a pioneer in education and one of my all-time personal heroes. Quite a bit of the book reflects his thinking. Another major influence was Professor

Bob McKim, a colleague and friend. We logically should have written this book together. However, Bob had just completed an excellent book of his own and was temporarily down with an overexposure to writing. Nonetheless, his influence and thoughts appear throughout. Bob also had the stamina to read the manuscript, as did Professor Harold Leavitt of the Stanford Graduate School of Business, an authority on organizational behavior, and Dr. James Fadiman, lecturer and resident psychologist of the Design Division. Cynthia Fry Gunn, my editor, transformed the manuscript into readable prose and selected the art work which adorns the following pages. Special thanks are due to Brooks/Cole Publishing Company for permitting the use of material contained in McKim's *Experiences in Visual Thinking*.

Thinking is not yet fully understood. You will therefore find material in this book based on unproven theory, conjecture, and non-scientific observation. Feel free to disagree with it if you would like to, because the intent of the book is not to deliver to you the last word in psychological theory. Its aim is rather to let you learn something about how your own mind works in a conceptual situation and to give you some hints on how to make it work better. This is, accordingly, a "think along" book, since it is difficult to talk about thinking without observing one's own thoughts. It is also a book that will, I hope, stimulate you to dig deeper into the game of thinking, with resulting benefits to your own idea-having capability.

James L. Adams
Stanford, California
March 5, 1974

## NOTE TO THE SECOND EDITION

A chapter has been added on groups and organizations, additional material has been added on perception, and the content has been somewhat updated. However, the basic message of the book and much of the original material remain unchanged.

J. L. A.
July 11, 1979

## NOTE TO THE THIRD EDITION

It's been over ten years since *Conceptual Blockbusting* was first published. I am even more convinced of the value of consciously identifying conceptual blocks than I was when I originally wrote the book. The process is not only interesting in its own right, but is a powerful tool in increasing creativity. As we enter the latter half of the nineteen-eighties, it is becoming increasingly clear that new ways of thinking and of engendering creativity need to become a natural part of the way we live.

We are quite programmed in our thinking for a number of good reasons, and tend to have well-developed thinking styles. Therefore we all have conceptual blocks. However, we are fortunately blessed with the ability to consciously modify our problem-solving habits in order to arrive at more creative inputs. In order to do this we must acquire increased awareness of our problem-solving process. We need to become suspicious of our business-as-usual habits and learn to better recognize when we should modify them. We need to learn more about the details of creative problem-solving. This book, with its emphasis on mental blocks, is an effective way toward such self-knowledge since conceptual blocks are universal, easily identifiable, and can, with effort, be modified.

Everyone wants to be more creative (or thinks they do). Motivation is not a problem. An understanding of conceptual blocks can only increase your motivation, simply because these blocks are not consistent with your self image (Who, me? Stereotype? No way!). In addition to this internal motivation, life seems to give us many additional reasons to be creative. The combination of motivation and conscious intervention based on increased awareness and knowledge of the problem-solving process is the standard formula for increasing creativity. This book seems to be successful enough in helping people accomplish this that I am not about to make major changes in its message.

For this third edition, I have updated the material and expanded the final chapter. In particular, I have included more discussion of the relative roles of internal and external motivation in creativity, since I'm convinced that the only way to become a consistently better problem-solver is to understand both the how *and* why of creativity.

J. L. A.
October 15, 1985

## NOTE TO THE FOURTH EDITION

Little did I think when I originally put this book together that I would be revising it on its 25th birthday. Happy birthday, *Conceptual Blockbusting*! I would like to think its relatively long life is a tribute to my writing talent, but I am afraid I must admit that the answer lies in the content.

Creativity is a critical factor in our success and happiness and the book is about common mental blocks that impede creative ideas (hence conceptual blocks). A better understanding of such blocks and ways to handle them helps us in life. As an added attraction, these blocks are in themselves fascinating. They both hamper us and help us. They restrict our abilities to solve our problems in original and more effective ways, but without them we would be less stable and predictable and perhaps less efficient at routine living. Our brains would be forced to process more information and our behavior might be more bothersome to those around us.

Since this book has been quite well-received by those involved in this quest, I did not radically re-orient it in this edition. I added quite a bit of information—some from new insights into the brain and how it works and some from the large amount of study of groups and organizations that has been done in the last dozen years. I also updated the book, since much has changed since the last edition. The cold war has ended, we are a more global society, economic and political alignments and demographics have changed, life has become increasingly affected by digital communications and information processing, and as I shall mention in Chapter 1, we have learned quite a bit more about how we think and solve problems and about creativity. But despite these changes, conceptual blocks continue to play their same role in inhibiting our creativity. May this book help you better understand and manage them.

Writing a book does not happen in a vacuum. In addition to all of the people who have influenced and taught me over the years (and that would be a book in itself) I would like to thank Nick Philipson, Marco Pavia, Marisa Kutner, and the other people at Perseus who shepherded this edition into reality. They were wonderful to work with and amazingly able to remain calm as I nitpicked my way through many iterations. As always I also want to thank my beloved wife Marian, my at-home critic, copy editor, cheerleader, and disciplinarian

J. L. A.

# ILLUSTRATIONS AND QUOTATIONS

Page vi: MAGRITTE, René. *The Thought Which Sees*. 1965. Graphite on paper, 15 ? x 11 ?" (40 x 29.7 cm). The Museum of Modern Art, New York. Gift of Mr. and Mrs. Charles B. Benenson. Photograph „ 2001 The Museum of Modern Art, New York.

Page xvi: M.C. Escher's *Belvedere* © 2001 Cordon Art B.V. – Baarn – Holland. All rights reserved.

Page 2: Arnold Palmer "Athlete of the Decade" illustration. ARNOLD PALMER © UFS. Reprinted by Permission.

Page 9: Goldberg, Rube. *Be Your Own Dentist*. © 1930. Pen and Ink. Rube Goldberg is the , and „ of Rube Golberg Inc.

Page 10: Drawing by Jim M'Guinness. Other drawings by Jim M'Guinness are found on pages 27, 28, 58, 100, 101, 136, 137.

Page 14: Lichtenstein, Roy. *Cathedral, #5*. 1969. Two-color lithograph. © Estate of Roy Lichtenstein.

Page 14: Paradoxical figures from *Eye and Brain* by R.L. Gregory, Mc-Graw-Hill Paperbacks. © 1966 R. L. Gregory. Courtesy of the author.

Page 14: "Three Legged Pants" illustration. Courtesy of Levi Strauss & Co., San Francisco.

Page 18: Swarm of A's. Illustration by Carol Leudesdorf.

Pages 22 & 23: Drawings from Creative Behavior Workbook by Sidney J. Parnes. Used by permission of Charles Scribner's Sons. Copyright © 1967 Charles Scribner's Sons.

Page 22: Nicholason, Karl. Volkswagen drawing from CRM Books, *Involvement in Developmental Psychology Today*. © 1971, CRM. Reprinted by permission of Random House, Inc.

Page 38: Picabia, Francis. *Parade Amoureuse*, 1917. © 2001 Artists Rights Society (ARS), New York / ADAGP, Paris.

Page 43: de CHIRICO, Giorgio. *The Anxious Journey*. 1913. Oil on canvas, 29 ? x 42" (74.3 x 106.7 cm). The Museum of Modern Art, New York. Acquired through the Lillie P. Bliss Bequest. Photograph „ 2001 The Museum of Modern Art, New York.

Page 47: Unknown artist. 18th century. *Victorian Making His Flight*. Frontispiece of Restif de la Bretonne, *La Decouverte australe, par un Hommevolant* . . . Leipzig, 1781. Engraving. Courtesy of Rare Book Division, The New York Public Library, Astor, Lenox and Tilden Foundations.

Page 52: Hogarth, William. *False Perspectives*. Published in *The Works of William Hogarth, from the Original Plates Restored by James Heath*. Printed for Baldwin & Cradock, by G. Woodfall, London, 1835. Courtesy of Special Collections, University of Michigan, Ann Arbor.

Page 56: Tycho Brahe's quadrant, c.1576. Illustration from Tycho Brahe's *Astronomiae Instaurate Mechanicae*, 1602. Courtesy of Science Museum Library, London. British Crown Copyright.

Page 60: Seymour, Robert (Shortshanks.). British, 1798-1836. *Locomotion*. Cartoon, hand-colored etching. Courtesy of the Metropolitan Museum of Art, Gift of Paul Bird, Jr., 1962.

Page 76: Christo. *5,600 Cubic Meter Package*. Project. 1967. Pencil on paper. Collection Kimiko and John Powers, New York. (Photo and © by Harry Shunk.)

Page 96: Christo. *Deux Chaises et Table Empaquetées, Projet pour le Model Usine Spectrum, Bergeyk, Hollande*. Collage 1965. 113 x 74 x 5 cm. (44 ? x 29 1/8 x 2"). Pencil, polyethylene, rope, twine, enamel paint, acrylic paint, charcoal, cardboard and wood. COPYRIGHT CHRISTO 1965. Private collection USA.

Page 107: Drawing courtesy of Walter Thomason, San Francisco.

Page 107: Drawings courtesy of Peter Dreissigacker, Stanford.

Page 124: Myers Briggs Illustration. Reprinted by permission of Harvard University Press, Cambridge, MA. From *Flying Buttresses, Entropy, and O-Rings* by James L. Adams. Copyright „1991 by the President and Fellows of Harvard College.

# Conceptual
# Blockbusting

## CHAPTER ONE

# Introduction

OUR LEARNING CAPACITY is truly impressive, not only in terms of knowledge, but also in terms of function. The amount of information the brain can retain is phenomenal. However, so is its ability to control the actions of the juggler, the stunt pilot, or the musician. Some of our functions, such as circulating blood and sensing temperature, although magnificent in complexity, are automatic in that they do not require conscious learning. Others, such as running and vocalizing, are easily, almost naturally acquired, yet demand considerable conscious effort if a level of excellence is to be attained. Still others, such as tennis, leather tanning, espaliering, chess playing, hang-gliding, and reading, must be acquired through conscious effort.

What about thinking? It is certainly a most important function. Is it automatic? Is it learned consciously? The time-honored method of improving one's skill is to be continually conscious of one's performance and to seek to improve it—usually according to an ideal or standard of what is desirable. The serious golf player studies golf and then continually practices, comparing his performance and form against an ideal, reading books and newspaper columns on golf form, and watching other more sophisticated golfers as they play.

Should the thinker act like this? Should we learn all we can about thinking and then practice and monitor our result? Should we compare our thinking with that done by more sophisticated thinkers? I began the previous editions of this book with the bit of antiquity shown on the next page, part of a series designed to help golfers improve their performance. Although to my knowledge Tiger Woods has not published his equivalent, the world abounds with material on how to play sports, cook, grow

## *Arnold Palmer*

"ATHLETE OF THE DECADE"

### ROLL INSIDE ON LEFT FOOT

The manner in which you lift your left foot during your backswing influences the success of your over-all swing.

If you go up on the toe of this foot, as the golfer in illustration No. 1 is doing, you react in a reverse manner on

your downswing. You will lower the heel in a manner that shifts weight to the back of this foot. This could cause you to fall back on your heels.

If you roll onto the inside of your left foot during your backswing, however (illustration No. 2), you will tend to react on your downswing by shifting your weight to the left (illustration No. 3). This is the proper weight transfer that is so necessary for consistent shot-making.

®, ©        NAT'L. News. Syn.

plants, build houses, fix plumbing, develop magnificent abs, and use Photoshop.

Have you ever seen a similar treatment of thinking? All of us are thinkers. However, most of us are surprisingly unconscious of the process of our own thinking. When we speak of *improving the mind* we are usually referring to the acquisition of information or knowledge, or to the *type* of thoughts one *should* have, and not to the actual *functioning* of the mind. We spend little time monitoring our own thinking and comparing it with a more sophisticated ideal.

## Thinking Form

There are reasons for this, of course. Thinking "form" is much more difficult to observe than, say, golfing "form." Thinking is also a much more complex function than golf. If you were to write the thinking analogue to the golf column, how could you select the "thinker of the decade" and how could you extract as simple an element as the role of the left foot from the complex process of thinking? Yet, despite these problems, effort spent in monitoring the thinking process and attempting to improve it is a good investment for the problem-solver.

We know a lot more about thinking, creativity, and problem solving than we did when the first edition of this book appeared. We have seen photographs and TV images of PET (Positive Emission Tomography) scans showing activity location as the brain works on various problems. We have become familiar with drugs both legal (Prozac) and frowned upon (crack) that alter the function of the brain. Tremendous amounts of literature and software have appeared on problem-solving and creativity and a large number of consultants and "experts" on creativity and innovation occupy podiums and retreat centers across the land. The cognitive sciences have unlocked secrets of information processing in the brain and bio-chemists have learned much about the electro-chemical processes in the brain and nervous system. But despite what we may have learned from the "cognitive revolution," most of us continue to think in traditional and habitual ways.

Conceptual blocks still control us. Much of thinking is quite automatic. In previous editions of this book I used the word "unconscious" to describe thinking of which we are unaware. Many people who study the brain—especially those in the cognitive sciences—dislike this word, perhaps because it implies that there are things going on in the brain that cannot be understood. But since I am an engineer I will continue to use it. A couple of examples will demonstrate my point. However, before I give them to you, let me diverge a moment and make a general comment about this book. It contains occasional examples and exercises.

The content of the book is much more meaningful and much more likely to influence your thinking if the exercises and problems are worked. You can do this either alone or with other people. I have found that most of them are usually more entertaining and more successful if several people are involved. It is always of interest to see the variation in thinking among a number of people. Try the exercises on your friends and associates at whatever occasion may seem appropriate, whether they are reading the book or not. In any case, try to work them yourself. You will need only paper and pencil. It is surprisingly easy to read material about thinking, accept it intellectually, and yet not have one's own thinking processes affected. This book is a little bit like one about jogging. It won't do you nearly as much good unless you run a little.

Now, back to the examples. The following puzzle, which originates with Carl Duncker, is taken from *The Act of Creation* by Arthur Koestler. Work on it awhile. When you get the answer or get tired of thinking about it, proceed.

> **Puzzle:** "One morning, exactly at sunrise, a Buddhist monk began to climb a tall mountain. A narrow path, no more than a foot or two wide, spiraled around the mountain to a glittering temple at the summit. The monk ascended at varying rates of speed, stopping many times along the way to rest and eat dried fruit he carried with him. He reached the temple shortly before sunset. After several days of fasting and meditation he began his journey back along the same path, starting at sunrise and again walking at variable speeds with many pauses along the way. His average speed descending was, of course, greater than his average climbing speed. Prove that there is *a spot* along the path that the monk will occupy on both trips at precisely the same time of day."

Did you solve the puzzle? More importantly, for our purposes, can you remember *what thinking processes* you used in working on the puzzle? Did you verbalize? Did you use imagery? Mathematics? Did you consciously try different strategies or attacks on the problem? It is probable that you tried several methods of working the problem, but that your mind automatically switched from one to the other. You were probably not particularly aware of what mental processes you were employing as you thought about the problem. You were playing a game (like tennis) without being very aware of what you were doing or of techniques by which you could improve your game (like getting your racket back faster).

A simple way of solving the puzzle is to visualize the upward journey of the monk superimposed upon the downward journey. Visualize, if you would, two monks, one at the bottom of the path and one at the top as the sun is rising. Let the bottom monk duplicate the upward journey as the upper monk duplicates the downward journey. It should be apparent that at some time and at some point on the path they will collide. This point is the spot along the path and the time of the collision is the time.

If you happened to choose visual imagery as the method of thinking to apply to this problem, you probably solved it. (A slightly more abstract approach is to imagine a plot on a graph of each monk's position as a function of time. The two lines will necessarily cross at a common position and time.) If you chose verbalization, you probably did not solve the problem. In fact, even after knowing the visual solution, if you revert to a verbal attack, the problem becomes confusing again. If you attempted an abstract mathematical approach that did not involve graphing, you probably once again failed to solve the problem and expended much more effort than was necessary.

As another example before you turn the page determine how you would complete the sequence below:

$$\frac{\text{A} \qquad \text{EF}}{\text{BCD} \qquad \text{G}}$$

In other words, how would you place the remaining letters of the alphabet above and below the line to make some kind of sense to you?

Unless you were suspicious that you were being tricked or that there was a "correct" answer, you probably reached a conclusion in a relatively short time. If you think about it, the task you performed was quite impressive. You needed to have knowledge (of alphabets and words), strategies (of patterns and general problem solving), and the ability to make some decisions. Yet you may have reached an answer in a few seconds. The mind is wonderful at handling uncertainty, forming patterns, and reaching decisions. You also probably arrived at a solution that satisfied you and then turned your attention away from the problem and back toward the text. This particular behavior is unconscious (Did you really brood about the suitability of your answer?) and has been called *satisficing*. It is characteristic of human behavior. The mind generally does not compulsively continue to unearth additional options. It sacrifices concepts in order to reach a speedy decision.

In one of his early works, Herbert Simon characterized a satisficer as one who stopped looking through a haystack when he found a needle. An optimizer, on the other hand, would take the whole haystack apart looking for all possible needles in order to be able to pick the sharpest one. Obviously life does not allow us time to completely disassemble all of the haystacks we encounter. However, and this is pertinent to problem solving, our natural behavior may often lead us to the less than sharpest needle.

I have used the ABC problem often with many individuals and groups. They reach an answer in a short time and then satisfice. Some of their answers are summarized here:

A. *Group size*

| | | | | | | | |
|---|---|---|---|---|---|---|---|
| 1. A | EF | HIJ | | 1 | 2 | 3 | etc. |
| BCD | | G | KL | 3 | 1 | 2 | |

| | | | | | | |
|---|---|---|---|---|---|---|
| 2. A | EF | KLM | | 1 | 2 | 3 | etc. |
| BCD | GHIJ | | | 3 | 4 | | |

   3. Random, all on top, all on bottom, or otherwise get it over with.

B. *Letter shapes*

   1. Letters with curved lines below; letters without curved lines above.

   2. Letters with crossbars above; letters without crossbars below.

   3. Letters below can be formed without lifting pencil from paper; letters above cannot.

C. *Sound*

   1. Top letters are soft; bottom letters are hard.

   2. Top letters would take the article *an;* bottom letters would take *a.*

   3. Top letters begin with vowel sound.

D. *Miscellaneous*

| | | | |
|---|---|---|---|
| 1. A | EF | IJK | (Top groups begin with vowels.) |
| BCD | GH | | |

   2. Move BCDG up and put all on top (or move AEF down and put all on bottom).

3. People have sung it to me (letters correspond to musical notes).
4. Bottom letters seem warmer (more friendly).
5. Top letters are easier to type.
6. Top letters are initials of western industrialized countries (America, England, France); bottom letters are initials of non-industrialized countries.
7. Top letters are all in "elephant" (wrong, but wonderful).

What are your reactions to these? Are any of them amusing? Annoying? Wrong? Can you guess why you react the way you do? The answer probably has to do with the fact that you did not think of them. If you satisficed, are you now less satisfied? It is often the case that we become less satisfied with our original answer if the problem seems to be turning into a contest. Satisficing seems to depend somewhat on the rules of the game, and a little conscious thinking can change these rules.

Finally, how did you arrive at the answer(s) you chose? Think about it a while. How much of the process was conscious? You probably remember some conscious thinking that occurred. How much was not conscious? You probably did not consciously pick the problem solving-strategy you used. Did the answer(s) merely "occur" to you? Your mind relied upon its familiar mix of conscious and unconscious activity.

Problem solving is quite habitual. We are all programmed in our thinking to a remarkable degree by genetics and by our life experience. If we are optimists, we suspect that habit must be beneficial in life. Not only is it beneficial, but also absolutely necessary to life as we know it. If we consider physical habits, our conscious abilities are simply not rapid enough to control our bodies as we play tennis, a piano concerto, or even walk, eat, or tie our shoes. It is fortunate for us that our brain has a subsystem called the cerebellum, which learns complex combinations of movements and plays them back when needed. These habits, most of which do not require much from our consciousness, allow us to live our complex physical lives.

Similarly, habits allow us to solve intellectual problems much more rapidly than we could if we had to rely completely upon consciousness. We look at $12 \times 12$ and 144 appears. We scan printed material and hear it being spoken. We look at a balance sheet and have a sense of the health of the company. We appraise a structure and know that it is a good design. We take one look at a patient and know she is not well. These things we do because we have constructions of knowledge and mental process that are available for our use when we need them. These constructions also minimize our intellectual risk since the ones we have are usually ones that have been tested and found to be successful in the past. In addition, they give us precision as we perform repetitive tasks. Habit, therefore, allows us to move rapidly, accurately, and safely. It would be impossible for us to complete our mental tasks without habit.

Habit also gives us stability. You would not think much of me if you met me each day and each time you met me I was using a totally different set of problem-solving habits. I would be unpredictable and possibly would be considered "insane." In a sense, a schizophrenic is one who discomforts us by constantly changing problem-solving habits. Neither could groups and large organizations acquire their character and uniqueness without habits. Companies worry about their "company culture," which depends on habits. Useful characteristics such as technical sophistication, marketing aggressiveness, and ability to weather economic downturns require habits. Finally, as we will see later, cognitive psychologists are not above counting bits and worrying about how we process information. This worry is a legitimate one because, in a sense, we have a one-watt mind in a megawatt world. We cannot process all of the data available to us in raw form. The mind, therefore, depends heavily on structures, models, and stereotypes. These are part and parcel of habit; without habit, we couldn't process the information we need in order to exist.

But, the news is not all good. Habits are often inconsistent with creativity. Creativity implies deviance from past procedure; habits are consistent with it. Habits often destroy creative ideas before they see the light of day. Habits include conceptual blocks, which not only occur because of the mechanisms of our limited brains, but are imparted by socialization, education, and professional specialization.

This book aims to make you more aware of what is going on in your mind (what you are doing) and to give you a few techniques (getting your racket back faster) which may improve your capability to solve problems (the game). We will be concentrating upon *conceptualization*, or the process by which one has ideas. This process is a key one in problem-solving, since the more creative concepts you have to choose from, the better. This is true at all stages of the problem-solving process, whether you are attempting to decide upon a broad direction or implement a detailed solution.

By concentrating on conceptualization, I am not attempting to downgrade the many other processes necessary in problem-solving, such as judgment, analysis, proper problem-definition, and the critical aspect of coaxing the idea into reality. Neither am I trying to insult your intelligence by pointing out the obvious value of a rich store of concepts to choose from. However, my work with students, professional people, and others over the years has convinced me that conceptualization does not always receive the attention it should in problem-solving. Conceptualization in problem-solving should be creative and should be treated as a major activity. Unfortunately, in actual problem-solving situations, people often fall short of this goal.

As mentioned earlier, the natural response to a problem seems to be to try to get rid of it by finding an answer—often taking the first answer that occurs and pursuing it because of one's reluctance to spend the time and mental effort needed to conjure up a richer storehouse of alternatives from which to choose. This hit-and-run approach to problem-solving begets all sorts of oddities—and often a chain of solution-causing-problem-requiring-solution, *ad infinitum.* In engineering one finds the "Rube Goldberg" solution, in which the problem is solved by an inelegant and complicated collection of partial solutions. I am sure that many of you are familiar with some example of this in the form of an appliance you have attempted to repair.

## Solutions to Problems That Don't Exist

In problem-solving, we also encounter solutions to problems that do not really exist. Remember the early (and unpopular) computer-generated voices in automobiles informing the operator of the state of the vehicle? I assume at least some of you have giggled at television spots of Andy Rooney pointing out useless features on appliances. I am presently looking at a kitchen blender whose buttons are marked mix, puree, grate, stir, liquefy, chop, blend, and whip. Care to put them in the proper order?

The objects represented in the drawing below were a lesson to me when I worked at the Jet Propulsion Laboratory long ago. They are devices to retard the opening of solar panels for spacecraft. The two on the right were developed by an extremely competent group (of which I was a part) in conjunction with the development of the Mariner IV, which was the first spacecraft to fly by Mars. The Mariner IV was to be provided with electrical power by four solar panels, which were to be latched together during launch, and then released and opened by spring-loaded actuators. Since there is no air in space to damp the opening of such panels and since they were covered with fragile and expensive solar cells, it was the custom to use a device to retard their opening.

The object on the left of the figure is such a device, which was used successfully on earlier lunar spacecraft. However, it was heavy and the designers of the Mars spacecraft did not trust it since it was filled with oil and had the potential of coating the spacecraft with a lethal layer of

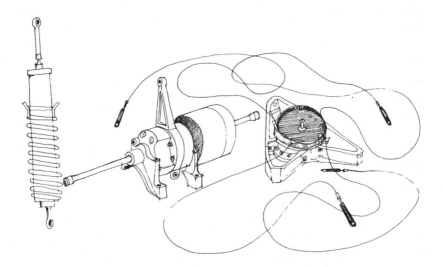

slime during the nine-month journey to Mars. The object in the middle of the drawing was the first solution to the problem. Unfortunately, although it contained no oil, it was extremely complex and was no lighter than the previous retarders. Its complexity and the results from a large amount of testing resulted in its rejection on the grounds of inadequate reliability.

The object on the right was the second solution. This was a central retarder that would control the opening speed of all four panels. Although it was filled with oil, the oil could not leak and the device was light in weight. However, it also proved to be unreliable as originally developed. At this point, full panic occurred in the program. There was no longer time to try a third approach, since planetary spacecraft cannot be delayed (the planet becomes much more difficult to reach until the next favorable alignment of the solar system, which usually does not occur for several years). An extremely expensive, around-the-clock emergency effort was therefore launched to increase the reliability of the damper, along with a simultaneous program of testing in order to measure the adverse effects of various malfunctions of the central retarder which might occur in flight.

One of the malfunctions investigated was that in which the retarder failed completely to retard. Amazingly enough, the results were acceptable. The retarders were not, in fact, necessary at all. It was possible to allow the panels to open free and to catch them with energy absorbers at the end of their travel. The final solution to the problem is therefore illustrated by the very *absence* of a fourth object in the figure, since Mariner IV went to Mars without retarders—the most elegant possible solution to the problem.

The moral in the story is obvious. The apparent shortage of time in the development of this project coupled with the natural desire of those involved to solve problems as quickly as possible resulted in overlooking alternative concepts (such as *no* retardation) that could have prevented the wild-goose chase.

Examples of the effects of the hit-and-run approach are as plentiful in other fields. Perhaps the most dramatic are hastily thought-out and implemented solutions that create more problems than they solve. Many examples of this have been given publicity in the environmental area and have resulted in the layers of regulation that now apply to anyone working on problems with environmental impact. Although this regulation annoys industry a great deal, it is beneficial since it requires that a large amount of effort be put into conceptualization before a solution is implemented. The amount of thought going into the disposition of nuclear waste would probably not occur without pressure and regulation and the quality of the solution will benefit from this conceptualization.

The ability to conceptualize productively and creatively is as important in painting the bathroom as in disposing of nuclear waste, in taking family vacations as in designing spacecraft, and in spending a family income as in protecting the environment. I am convinced that the conceptual process is a general one and that the same problems arise in thinking up a more nutritional diet as in thinking up a better way to image the heart ultrasonically.

Thinking well (once again, like playing tennis well) requires that many decisions be made unconsciously. One can no more think well by consciously picking each strategy and writing each sentence out longhand in the mind than one can play tennis well by consciously thinking of what position to place each joint in the body as one attempts to reach a difficult shot. However, just as tennis benefits from your becoming so familiar with various strategies that they become automatic, so does thinking.

As the book proceeds, I will attempt to make you more conscious of the creative process, various blocks that inhibit it, and various tricks that can augment it. Although this is not a psychology book, some of the theory underlying creativity will be briefly explored. These theoretical explications, although interesting, are incomplete. Hence, there is no specific thinking pattern that can make everyone into a super-conceptualizer. Some techniques and approaches work effectively for some people and yet fill others with loathing. If you come up against techniques or exercises that do nothing for you, plunge on. You will (I hope) soon find techniques and exercises that prove interesting to you.

A question that always arises when one approaches the *teaching* of creativity is "Can it be taught?" Obviously I think that it can be, or I would not be writing this book. The teaching may be more of an *encouraging,* but call it what you will, I am convinced that our efforts at Stanford result in an improvement in the quality of conceptual output from our students. Another question that often comes up is "Can't conscious efforts to be creative interfere with the creative process?" This will be dealt with more thoroughly in Chapter Three but, in brief, the answer is simple. If Leonardo da Vinci happens to be reading this book he is probably wasting his time. However, most of us are not Leonardos.

One of the earliest theories about creativity considers it to be a divine spark. Plato, in III, Ion, says about poets:

And for this reason God takes away the minds of these men and uses them as his ministers, just as he does soothsayers and goodly seers in order that we who hear them may know that it is not they who utter these words of great price when they are out of their wits, but that it is God himself who speaks and addresses us through them.

However, for most of us, creativity is more of a dull glow than a divine spark. And the more fanning it receives, the brighter it will burn.

## Conceptual Blocks

Let me now make a few comments about the framework of this book. Chapters Two through Five will be concerned with conceptual blocks: *mental walls that block the problem-solver from correctly perceiving a problem or conceiving its solution.* Everyone has them. However, they vary in quantity and in intensity from individual to individual. Most of us are not aware of the extent of our conceptual blocks. Awareness can not only allow us to better know our strengths and weaknesses, but can give us the motivation and the knowledge necessary to modify or avoid such blocks. These four chapters will discuss conceptual blocks, giving examples and exploring their causes. The blocks are closely related, as you will see when you begin to consider them. The particular scheme used to categorize them is for convenience only, and is not meant to be the ultimate morphology of conceptual blocks. Once again, please do the exercises and problems. The only way you will identify your own conceptual blocks is to try activities that are impeded by their existence.

Chapters Six and Seven are concerned with *techniques* that allow you to overcome (or sidestep) these blocks. Chapter Eight deals with conceptualization in a group setting. Chapter Nine examines a few blocks to creativity at the organizational level. The final section of the book, the Reader's Guide, contains information for those interested in pursuing this subject in greater depth. A great deal of material exists on creativity and conceptualization, and most of it is accessible without a specialist's vocabulary. I recommend it as not only fascinating, but also unique in that you are simultaneously able to acquire knowledge and improve your idea-having and problem-solving capability.

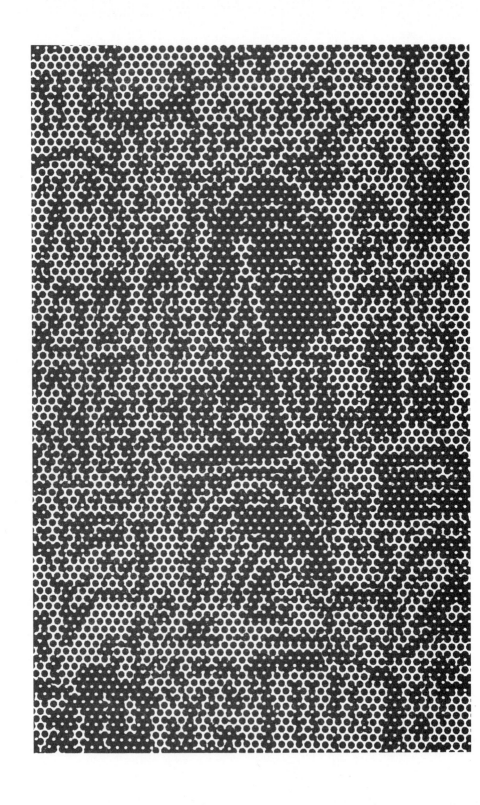

## CHAPTER TWO

# Perceptual Blocks

PERCEPTUAL BLOCKS ARE OBSTACLES that prevent the problem-solver from clearly perceiving either the problem itself or the information needed to solve the problem. Perhaps the best way of helping you overcome perceptual blocks is to talk about some common and specific ones.

## One: Detecting What You Expect—Stereotyping

We are continually reminded of the existence of stereotyping. Members of ethnic minorities, women, homosexuals, the elderly, the disabled, and others have successfully taught us that social stereotypes are wrong. Yet stereotypes continue to play a large role in our lives. If you are male, imagine the effect on people's perception of you if you were to wear high-heeled shoes. If you are a woman, just wear a fake mustache the next time you go into a job interview. Stereotyping and labeling are extremely prevalent and effective perceptual blocks. The simple truth of the matter is, you cannot see clearly if you are controlled by preconceptions. And evidence that violates preconceptions, although perhaps initially interesting or amusing, is often rejected, as you might be with your high heels or fake mustache.

As another example of the power of stereotyping, I wear neckties. I do not like them and at one time considered never wearing them again. However, I decided that this was a foolish battle, because the stereotyping associated with a necktie is so strong that I can accomplish certain things professionally much easier by wearing one, since people assume I am more important.

Perceptual stereotyping is part of the explanation for the success of various types of optical trickery such as in the figures on the next page.

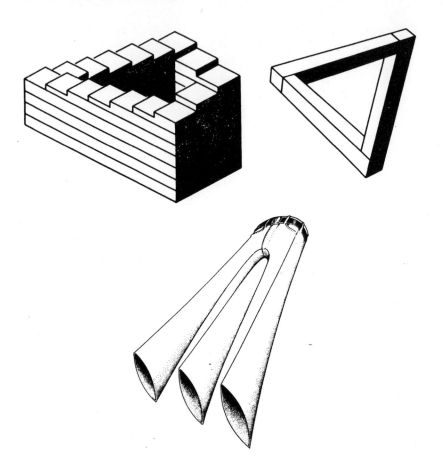

Perceptual stereotyping is not all bad, since it also allows people to complete incomplete data. However, it can be a serious handicap to perceiving new combinations. Creativity has sometimes been called the combining of seemingly disparate parts into a functioning and useful whole. Stereotyped conceptions of the parts hinder their combination into a new whole, where the roles they play may be quite different.

Once a label (professor, housewife, black, chair, butterfly, automobile, laxative) has been applied, people are less likely to notice the actual qualities or attributes of what is being labeled. For instance, say I am trying to think of what to do with a warehouseful of chairs. If I can think of them only as chairs, I can probably only come up with such uses as sitting on them, standing on them, or hitting villains with them in grade-B movies. But if I think of the attributes of the chairs (fabric, padding, wooden legs, screws, and so on), I can come up with many more uses. Maybe I should take the chairs apart and sell the seats to people who attend football games, make purses from the leather back covering, sell the screws as surplus hardware, and sell the wood to home craftsmen. Stereotyping inhibits this type of thinking.

Unfortunately, stereotyping is inherent in the working of the mind. Much of the information used in conceptualizing is first recorded in the memory and later recalled, rather than used immediately upon acquisition. The memory cannot retain all of the raw information that comes in through the senses. The mind therefore processes it by filtering out what is judged to be less useful and categorizing the rest to be as consistent as possible with information already stored in the memory. When the information is later recalled, it is in a simplified and regularized form—in a sense, a stereotype of the original.

Although the mechanisms of memory are not completely understood, there seem to be at least three mechanisms at work, one which holds incoming information for a fraction of a second in the form received from the body's sensors while a pattern-recognition process can take place that reduces the information to a more conceptual form.

For example, the pattern-recognition function in your mind allows you to discern the letter "a" from the myriad of forms that appear on page 18 (this is obviously a sophisticated process).

After the information is reduced to a more conceptual form, it goes into the short-term memory (STM). STM is much more limited in the amount of information it is able to store, but it can hold this information for a greater length of time (several seconds). This mechanism, for instance, holds the telephone number you get from the information operator until you punch the proper buttons. If you don't either rapidly use it or do something such as write it down or repeat it to yourself, it disappears.

Although STM is extremely important in carrying out our daily activities, we are particularly interested in long-term memory (LTM), which allows us to solve problems, gives us our sense of self, and enables us to communicate sensibly. Only a small portion of the information that enters our sensory register and filters through STM ends up in LTM. *Attention* provides the focusing mechanism of LTM. While performing the complex tasks of living (such as driving to work in the morning), LTM is attending to only a small fraction of the inputs from the senses. Most of these inputs merely cycle through STM.

It is the material already in LTM that determines attention; the mind

tends to reinforce what is already there. For instance, if you are an oenophile, you will record a great deal of new material you encounter on wine to add to your already considerable store of knowledge. Similarly, you will record very little information on a topic you dislike. If you hate math, you will record little new math-related information. This tendency should make you suspicious as to whether material you recall from your memory contains an honest representation of detail that is unpleasant to you. (It does not.) It should also make you suspect that stereotyping is particularly strong in areas that have been unimportant to you and/or unpleasant for you to think about. (It is.)

Information reaching LTM must be filed, and this process depends on context. The following exercise illustrates this:

**Exercise:**
Remember the following list. Read it and close the book. Then see if you can repeat it to yourself.

saw, when, panicked, Jim, ripped, haystack, the, relaxed, when, cloth, the, but, he

I assume that this was not only difficult, but also that your brain resisted such an apparently useless exercise. However, I will now make these words into a relatively meaningless sentence and, although the sentence may seem both dumb and amusing, you will be able to remember it more easily.

**Exercise:**
Remember the following sentence. Read it and close the book. Then see if you can repeat it to yourself.
Jim panicked when the cloth ripped, but relaxed when he saw the haystack.

However, your brain, although more cooperative, still is not completely satisfied. It seeks meaning or consistence with some logical structure already within memory. I can give your brain this meaning through a simple phrase—parachute jumping. You have a structure for parachute jumping that will make the sentence meaningful, and when you now return and read it again, you will be happy. Also you will be more easily able to remember the sentence over a long period. See if you can recall it when you awaken tomorrow morning.

In this exercise, the information you originally saw was of little use to you since it was out of context. Your brain does not like to transfer this type of information to long-term memory, because it seems random rather than important. However, the "clues" from context you already possessed made it easy to "solve the problems" and transfer the information to your long-term memory.

Context is a key element in many memory techniques. One of the best known of these is the "method of loci." In this technique you first take a familiar walk and remember a number of scenes from the walk. To remember a number of items, superimpose a visual image of an item on each of the walk scenes. Recall then requires only mentally retracing the walk. Try it. This technique is surprisingly effective, especially for people with good visual-imagery ability. It is rumored that Cicero used this method to remember his orations to the Roman senate. It is further rumored that the technique is the origin of the phrase "in the first place we find …, in the second place we find …, etc." Probably not true, but it is such a good rumor that it should be.

We usually remember information in context, and the context goes into our memory along with the information. When we later recall the information for use in problem-solving, the residual information and feelings from the original context tend to accompany it. This complicates the conceptual process, since the residual material must be dealt with. If your first introduction to organ music is at a funeral, it may be difficult later to think of using organ music in a joyful pageant. Organ music has been, in a sense, stereotyped.

Information is also filed in the memory in a structured way. It is arranged in categories according to likely associations. Think of the word "menu." What else comes to mind? Waiters? Candles? Wine? Napkins? Lots of forks? Other restaurant scenes? Did you think of a snake? What about a tractor? A snake or tractor is unlikely, since they are not in your "restaurant" file. The structured information in your memory is so important to you that you may dismiss information that is inconsistent with that which is already there. Psychologists write about an unpleasant internal state, called cognitive dissonance, that results from an inconsistency among a person's knowledge, feelings, and behavior. The individual attempts to minimize this dissonance. One way to do this is to devalue information that does not fit one's stereotype.

With this in mind, let's look a bit further at labeling as applied to people. We all have stereotypes about people, and these often lead to social and interpersonal problems. I am a professor. Most of you, having never met me, can conclude quite a bit about me from the label "professor" and your stereotyping ability. However, although some of the characteristics you attribute to me might be accurate, you would have trouble working or living with me with only that information, for I have my own particular group of characteristics. I am a grandfather, a good mechanic, machinist, cook, and carpenter, and married to a woman I love madly who is an educational consultant and wired to the world. I tend to be happier in rural environments than cities and like a great deal of contact with other people in my work but prefer a light social schedule. I have a bad knee, a messy office, gray hair, and a 1909 brown shingle house. I am 6'4", weigh 230, and have many hobbies including restoring old heavy equipment, backpacking, and aimlessly driving through back country. Although politically liberal and living in a politically correct area, I still drink scotch, eat beef, and enjoy dirty jokes. Oh yes, I am also a professional engineer, a retired professor, and a consultant. As I list these attributes, you should be able to move beyond your ideas of the stereotype to get a better feel for me as a person, and therefore be better able to interact with me. I have also enriched the stereotype you have of "professor" by adding information. Now you try it. In the following exercise, see how you label yourself and how people label you.

> **Exercise:** Find someone you do not know too well. Each of you think of, and tell the other, a label (a few words) that describes you. Spend half a minute or so considering what the other person's label means to you. Then spend five minutes verbally exchanging additional characteristics. Alternate and keep moving. Do not succumb to the temptation to small talk (thereby being witty and engaging) to avoid trading information. Do not question the other person and do not try to steer the conversation. Just swap information.

Did you find this exercise a quick way to find out information about another person? Many people do. However, did you also find it difficult? Even after having lived a reasonably long and rich life, people generally run short on characteristics after a few minutes and spend more effort in thinking up their own attributes than in listening to those of the other person. They also generally experience an overwhelming desire to small-talk. Did you?

In social and professional interactions we tend to stick to stereotypes and generalities, unless at some point it seems to our benefit to become specific about ourselves. The above exercise therefore invades our privacy, since it forces us to divulge information before we may be ready to do so. After this exercise is over, most participants agree that they know much more about the other person than they would have gleaned from the original label. They also gain a sense of the importance of their own stereotype to them, as well as a better feeling of how they cling to stereotypes to avoid taking social risk. As a final comment, the exercise also shows that we do not have a large store of characteristics about ourselves in our memory. If we did, the exercise would be much easier. We not only stereotype other people and things, but we stereotype ourselves. Stereotyping is an obvious perceptual block—perhaps the most important one. But there are others, and let's now discuss some of them.

## Two: Difficulty in Isolating the Problem

Can you tell what the illustration at the top of the next page is? If you have seen this before you probably have no trouble in discerning it. If you have not, try to identify the contents before you continue. (Answer is on page 23.)

Another puzzle such as this is the picture below. What is it?

It's a classic Volkswagon Beetle, of course.

Now that you have seen the answer, it should be easy to see the cow. This is typical of visual puzzles that require the solver to detect meaning in the midst of apparent chaos.

Problems we face may be similarly obscured by either inadequate clues or misleading information. And proper problem-identification is of extreme importance in problem-solving. If the problem is not properly isolated, it will not be properly solved. Successful medical diagnosis depends on the ability to isolate the problem within the complexity of all of the real and imaginary information available to the physician. Successful coexistence between parents and teenage children requires the ability to isolate the real problems among many of the apparent ones.

Is your problem really a bad tank of gas, or does your car need timing or perhaps new distributor points? Or is your problem a living situation that makes you overly dependent upon a car? Problem statements are often liberally laced with answers. The answers may be well thought out or poorly conceived. They may be right or wrong. A problem statement to an architect such as "put a latch on that door between the kitchen and the dining room so that the door can be opened extremely easily" implies that the answer to kitchen/dining room access is a door, rather than no door, a redefinition of space, or a redefinition of the food preparation/eating function.

If you are working as a professional problem-solver, you must continually be alert to properly perceive the problem. The client, patient, customer, etc. may not always see the problem clearly, and the problem-solver is sometimes able to score heavily by curing the difficulties in a simpler manner through a clearer perception of what the problem really is. In engineering, people occasionally become so involved in attempting to optimize a particular device that they lose sight of alternate ways to alleviate the difficulty. Much thinking went into the mechanical design of various types of prototype tomato pickers before someone decided that the real problem was not in optimizing these designs but rather in the susceptibility of the tomatoes to damage during picking. The answer to the problem was a new plant, with tougher-skinned, more accessible fruit.

Jerry Porras, who is a professor in the Stanford Graduate School of Business, wrote an excellent little book entitled *Stream Analysis* some years ago. In this book he claims that people, especially people in organizations, tend to work on getting rid of symptoms, rather than solving the real problems. I used to assign this book to my students and ask them to do an analysis of their own problem-solving. After this exercise they were forced to agree with the thesis in the book, but were sure that this could not possibly be the case in big-time corporations. Shortly after that, I had the good fortune to join Jerry in a workshop for one of those very same big-time corporations in which he went through the problem-analysis approach in his book (I shall say more about it in Chapter 7). The results were overwhelming. We ended the exercise with some very bothered executives, who had been forced to realize that they were indeed ignoring the core problems. Not surprising, since core problems are more difficult to solve and their solution often creates greater controversy. But perhaps not what we would like to think.

Problems are, of course, often constrained by considerations other than mere removal of a difficulty, and the problem-solver must be sensitive to this. Assume, for instance, that I am a consulting engineer retained to help in the design of an improved product by a company that was a leading manufacturer of mechanical equipment used to clear clogged drains and sewers. Assume further that I perceive the problem to be a general one of unclogging drains and sewers. This might lead me to a very elegant solution (a mixture of commonly available chemicals) that would make obsolete the product line of the company and that would not take advantage of the company's field of competence. Although I could then proudly take my place among successful conceptualizers, my employer would probably not enjoy paying me. Properly isolating the problem is, of course, equally (or more) important if you are both problem-stater and problem-solver. Difficulty in isolating the problem is often due to the tendency to spend a minimum of effort on problem-definition in order to get to the important matter of solving it. Inadequately defining the problem is a tendency that is downright foolish on an important and extensive problem-solving task. A relatively small time spent in carefully isolating and defining the problem can be extremely valuable both in illuminating possible simple solutions and in ensuring that a great deal of effort is not spent only to find that the difficulties still exist—perhaps in even greater magnitude.

> **Exercise:** Think of a problem that is bothering you. State your problem in writing as concisely as you can. Can you think of alternative problem statements that might be causing the difficulties you are experiencing? If so, write them down and conjecture about the possible differences in solutions that occur to you.

### Three: Tendency to Delimit the Problem Area Poorly

Just as it is sometimes difficult to isolate the problem properly, it is also difficult to avoid delimiting the problem too closely. (In other words, one should not impose too many constraints upon it.) The following common puzzle is an example of this tendency to delimit too closely.

> **Puzzle:** Draw no more than four straight lines (without lifting the pencil from the paper) which will cross through all nine dots.

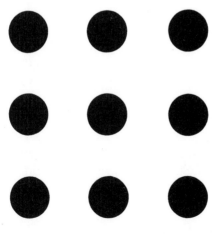

This puzzle is difficult to solve if the imaginary boundary (limit) enclosing the nine dots is not exceeded. One possible answer is shown below:

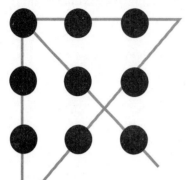

A surprising number of people will not exceed the imaginary boundary, for often this constraint is unconsciously in the mind of the problem-solver, even though it is not in the definition of the problem at all. The overly strict limits are a block in the mind of the solver. The widespread nature of this block is what makes this puzzle classic.

Such blocks are subtle and pervasive, but let me talk more about this puzzle to demonstrate that awareness of blocks can and often does result in the ability and motivation to overcome them. I used to use this puzzle years ago when I first came to Stanford in order to demonstrate conceptual blocks. For a talk which I once gave on the subject of problem-solving, an announcement was sent out with this puzzle on the cover. An anonymous party (confess) sent back this solution:

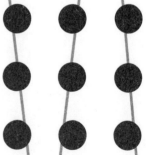

I officially designated him/her our official conceptual smart-ass and secretly admired that person because I was, of course, too blocked to realize that it wasn't necessary to draw the lines through the centers of the dots.

To add insult to this injury, one of my oldest friends later sent me the fiendish solution shown here, which allows all nine dots to be crossed off by one straight line—plus a little unblocked paper folding. Try this solution yourself—make a copy of the following page and start folding!

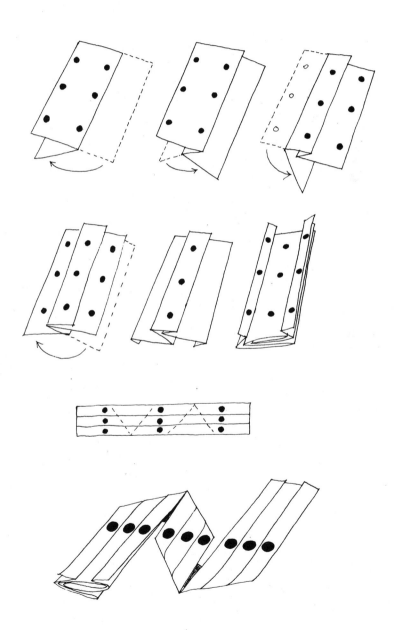

Fiendish Solution by Rodney W. Supple

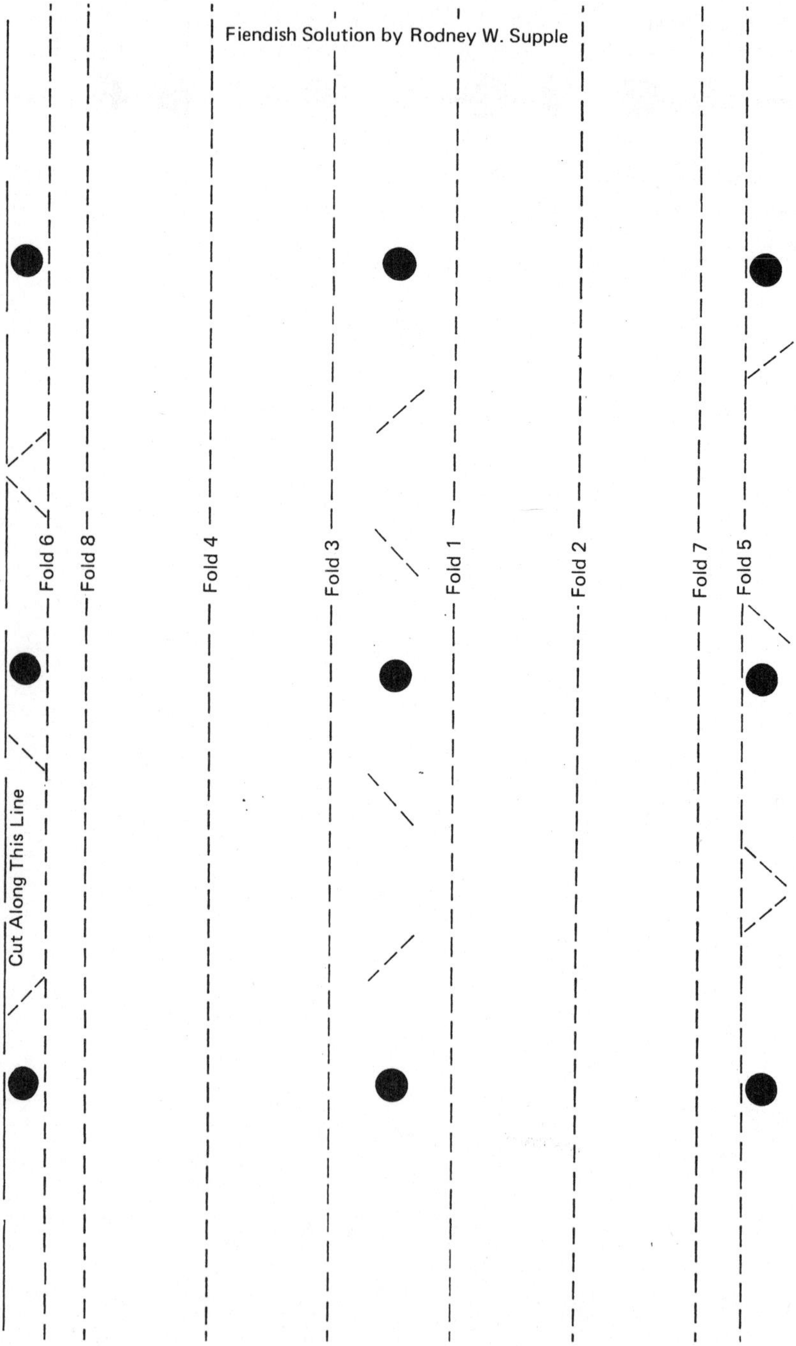

Cut Along This Line

Fold 6

Fold 8

Fold 4

Fold 3

Fold 1

Fold 2

Fold 7

Fold 5

I received many such as the one below, which merely requires cutting the puzzle apart, taping it together in a different format, and again using one line.

It is also possible to roll up the puzzle and draw a spiral through the dots (below), cut out the dots and shove the line through them, or otherwise violate the two-dimensional format.

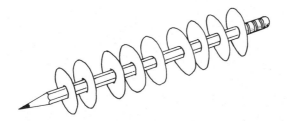

1 Line 0 Folds

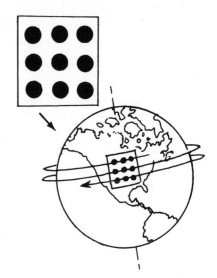

Lay the paper on the surface of the Earth. Circumnavigate the globe twice + a few inches, displacing a little each time so as to pass through the next row on each circuit as you "Go West, young man."

~ 2 Lines* 0 Folds

*Statistical

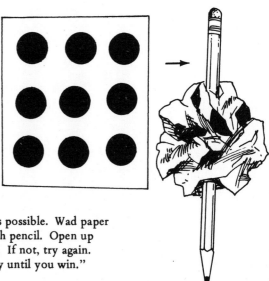

Draw dots as large as possible. Wad paper into a ball. Stab with pencil. Open up and see if you did it. If not, try again. "Nobody loses: Play until you win."

Solutions continue to roll in. My all-time favorite is the letter on the next page. By now I have received dozens of answers to this puzzle, all exceedingly clever and all depressing in that I had thought of none of them. Not only that, but Becky Buechel herself (the author of the classic which follows) ended up in my classroom at one point—small world.

Outbursts of creativity such as these are exciting. One of the messages of this book is that we place limits upon our own functioning (the

May 30, 1974
5 FDR Navasa
Roosevelt Rds.
Ceiba, P.R. 00635

Dear Prof. James L. Adams,
    My dad and I were doing Puzzles from "Conceptual Blockbusting". We were mostly working on the dot ones, like
::: My dad said a man found a way
:::
to do it with one line. I tried and did it. Not with folding, but I used a fat line. I doesn't say you can't use a fat line.
                    Like this

P.S.
acctually you
need a very fat
writing apparatice

sincerely,
Becky Buechel
age: 10

fence around the dots) and that once we realize the existence of these limits we will be eager to escape and will no longer be as hampered by them. The nine-dot puzzle is certainly evidence of this phenomenon. Limits are negotiable.

Just as a solution is sensitive to the proper isolation of the problem, it is also sensitive to proper limitation (constraints). The framing of a problem has great influence on the solution of it. In general, the more broadly the problem can be stated, the more room is available for conceptualization. A request for the design of a better door will probably result in a rectangular slab with hinges and a handle. Is this what is wanted, or is the problem really a better way to get through a wall? A request for a better way to get through a wall releases one from the preconception of the rectangular slab that swings or slides. Students given this problem statement will come up with all manner of geometries for walls and openings, elastic diaphragms, mechanical shutters, curtains, and ingenious rotating and folding mechanisms. Is this what is wanted, or is the problem a better method of acoustical, visual, or environmental isolation? The solution of a laminar air curtain as is used to keep heat in stores or out of freezers while permitting free passage would not be likely to come from a harshly delivered "design a better door" problem statement.

If you hire an architect or a structural engineer or a lawyer, you are paying for expertise. It is therefore foolish to constrain a problem so closely ("Here is a floor plan and an elevation—build it") that you are not taking advantage of the professional's abilities. This principle applies equally if a single person is both stating the problem and solving it. A problem statement which is too limited inhibits creative ability.

It is, of course, possible to err in the opposite direction and not delimit the problem sufficiently. The resulting solution may be so general or basic as not to be useful. An automobile company looking for a better way to keep windshields clean cannot do much with a solution that does away with automobiles. The proper statement of a problem therefore becomes a critical art, since it enables the extraction of the maximum of creative thought from the solver while still delivering a useful answer. I would hazard a guess, however, that more problems are overly limited in statement than inadequately limited. Because of that feeling and because this is a book on creativity, imposing too many constraints is expressly stated here to be *verboten*.

> **Exercise:** The next time you have a problem, solve it. Then, at your leisure, list at least three different possible delimitations of the problem and answers you might have come up with in each case.

For instance, suppose that you are a relatively new mother who took time off from your job to have your baby and that you are now torn between work and spending more time with your child.

Problem solutions are of course affected by pragmatic concerns, such as money and support from others, but let's assume that in this case money is not a problem and you have support from your spouse and friends. You might formulate your problem as "choosing between being a professional woman and mother" and quit working outside the house in order to devote full time to your baby. (I am assuming that you would not give up your baby). Alternately, you might see your problem as "how can I continue to have the satisfaction of work and yet spend the time I want with my child?" This problem statement contains fewer limits and might lead to involving the father more in child care or another career which allows you to work more flexible hours, work at home, work part time, etc.

You might phrase your problem as "how can I ensure that my child will receive care that will best encourage its proper development?" This has even fewer limits and might cause you to work with other new mothers to set up an outstanding day-care cooperative.

You might decide that the problem is conflict between the natural role of mother and modern expectations that modern women should be respected professionals in the outside world. This might lead to conversations with other people in your situation, opinion makers, therapists, and educators, a decision that a major social problem exists, and you becoming a militant author and the organizer of a national effort devoted to helping women with new children escape this conflict.

As limits on problem-definition are relaxed, one usually becomes involved in interdisciplinary considerations: economic, political, and ethical. If you see your problem as simply "conforming with federal government smog regulations," your answer may be to put gadgets on existing engines. However, if you see your problem as "minimizing air pollution" you may consider entirely new concepts in transportation and will be involved in complex social as well as technical considerations.

## Four: Inability to See the Problem from Various Viewpoints

It is often difficult to see a problem from the viewpoint of all of the interests and parties involved. However, consideration of such view-points not only leads to a "better" solution to the problem, in that it pleases more interests and individuals, but it is also extremely helpful in conceptualizing. Certainly in a problem between two people, the ability to see the problem from the other's point of view is extremely important in keeping the tone of the debate within reasonable bounds of refinement. In many cases, no solution is possible until each person can gain a feeling for the viewpoint of the other. Most problem solutions affect people other than the solver, and their interests must be considered. The architect must view the design of his buildings from the perspectives of the clients, the builders, suppliers, architectural critics, and others in the profession as well as from his own. Designers of an automobile should worry about those who must manufacture, operate, and maintain their output. The property owner building a fence must consider the viewpoints not only of neighbors, the city council, visitors, the garbageman, and passing motorists who can no longer see around the corner, but also of nonhuman participants such as the lawn, which may die in the shade of the fence, and the neighborhood cats, who may sit on the fence to better communicate their wails of war and love.

**Exercise:** Think of an interpersonal problem you presently have. Write a concise statement of the problem as seen by each party involved. If possible show the statements to the corresponding parties and see if they agree with your interpretation of their perception of the problem.

In his book *New Think*, Edward de Bono talks about vertical and lateral thinking. Vertical thinking begins with a single concept and then proceeds with that concept until a solution is reached. Lateral thinking refers to thinking that generates alternative ways of seeing a problem before seeking a solution. At one point in his book, De Bono explained vertical and lateral thinking by referring to the digging of holes. He states:

> Logic is the tool that is used to dig holes deeper and bigger, to make them altogether better holes. But if the hole is in the wrong place, then no amount of improvement is going to put it in the right place. No matter how obvious this may seem to every digger, it is still easier to go on digging in the same place than to start all over again in a new place. Vertical thinking is digging the same hole deeper; lateral thinking is trying again elsewhere.

De Bono acknowledged advantages in digging in the same hole, admitting that "a half-dug hole offers a direction in which to expend effort." He elaborated, "No one is paid to sit around being capable of achievement. As there is no way of assessing such capability it is necessary to pay and promote according to visible achievements. Far better to dig the wrong hole (even one that is recognized as being wrong) to an impressive depth than to sit around wondering where to start digging." However, De Bono made the point that many holes are being dug to an impractical depth, many in the wrong place, and that breakthroughs usually result from someone abandoning a partly-dug hole and beginning anew in a different place.

## Five: Saturation

Saturation takes place with all sensory modes. If the mind recorded all inputs so that they were all consciously accessible, our conscious mind would be very full indeed. Many extremely familiar inputs are not recorded in a way that allows their simple recall.

**Exercise:** Without looking at one, draw the push buttons on an ordinary phone, placing the letters, numbers, and symbols in the proper location.

Very few people can do this succesfully, even though they spend great amounts of time using telephones. However, the mind does not hold onto the details on the buttons, since it does not have to. If they were not marked on the phone, the mind would store the information for easy recall.

As other examples of saturation, you might try to draw (without looking at them) the grill on your car, your lawn mower handle, or any other object that you see repeatedly, but whose visual details are unimportant to you. Like a phone, even though you might think that you know the details, you cannot produce them when desired. The trickiest aspect of saturation is that you think you have the data, even though you are unable to produce it when needed.

Visual saturation is a problem in art schools, because it is necessary to teach students to see things they are used to ignoring. For this reason, beginning art students are sometimes told to do things like bending over and looking at the world upside down, since this upside-down orientation makes visible details that are usually not noticed (try it). Similarly if you look away from a nice sunset you notice all manner of usually unnoticed visual activity in the easterly direction, such as colors on clouds, muted tones on buildings, reflected lights on windows, etc.

Another situation that requires attention to saturation in problem-solving occurs when data arrives only occasionally or in the presence of large amounts of distracting data. Radar inputs in the military or in air traffic control are an example of this, as are irregularities in the operation of an airplane or ground vehicle that appear after a long period of normal behavior. The life of a professional pilot, for instance, has occasionally been described as years of tedium interspersed with seconds of terror. When the information resulting in this terror becomes available, it is obviously extremely important that the pilot notice it as soon as possible. Fortunately for us passenger-types, a great amount of effort on the part of human—factors engineers, psychologists, and equipment designers—goes into ensuring that the tedium will be suitably interrupted.

## Six: Failure to Utilize all Sensory Inputs

The senses are interconnected in a fairly direct manner. This will be discussed further in Chapter Six. Senses such as sight and hearing and taste and smell are commonly linked. Taste is severely inhibited if smell is suppressed. Similarly sight is augmented in a major way by sound (motion pictures).

Various sensory inputs (notably vision) are important to people who are extremely innovative. This is amply recorded in the literature. In a letter to Jacques Hadamard (taken from *The Creative Process*, edited by

Brewster Ghiselin), Albert Einstein said: "The words or the language, as they are written or spoken, do not seem to play any role in my mechanism of thought. The psychical entities which seem to serve as elements in thought are certain signs and more or less clear images which can be 'voluntarily' reproduced and combined. . . . The above mentioned elements are, in my case, of visual and some of muscular type. Conventional words or other signs have to be sought for laboriously only in a secondary stage, when the mentioned associative play is sufficiently established and can be reproduced at will." Tesla, an extremely productive technological innovator (fluorescent lights, the A.C. generator, the "Tesla" coil), apparently had incredible visualization powers. As described by J. J. O'Neill in *Prodigal Genius: The Life of Nikola Tesla*, it was claimed that Tesla "could project before his eyes a picture complete in every detail, of every part of the machine. These pictures were more vivid than any blueprint." Further, Tesla claimed to be able to test his devices mentally, by having them run for weeks—after which time he would examine them thoroughly for signs of wear.

Problem-solvers need all the help they can get. They should therefore be careful not to neglect any sensory inputs. An engineer working on an acoustics problem for a concert hall, for instance, should not get so carried away with theoretical analysis that she neglects to look at a wide variety of concert halls and listen to the quality of sound in each. She must also be aware that her acoustical treatment, although successful to the ear, may overly offend the eye and, if her material choice is extreme enough, perhaps also the nose.

It is for this reason that designers sometimes will consciously deprive themselves temporarily of certain sensory inputs to make sure they have adequately recorded others. The designer of a patio cover intended to take the place of shade trees until they grow high enough in a new yard would be well advised not only to look at trees, but also to listen to them, feel them, smell them, climb them, and generally saturate himself with them for a good bit of time before starting the design. In a well-working marriage, one is sensitive not only to the appearance of one's partner, but also to the sound, smell, taste, and feel of him or her. Problems between the two are best solved by utilizing inputs from all of these senses.

Convincing students that they should use all of the sensory inputs at their disposal was one of my most difficult challenges when I taught design at Stanford University. My students were highly verbal (they are admitted to school that way) and were relatively less competent visually. They were not used to relying on taste, smell, or feel for problem-solving. Generally speaking, they were familiar with problems that can be solved (they thought) verbally or mathematically. They were not used to using sensory imagery in their thinking. This subject will be covered in more detail in Chapter Six, so we will dwell no more on it here. Suffice it to say that failure fully to utilize inputs from all the senses is a conceptual block that is quite common in problem-solving.

PARADE AMOUREUSE

## CHAPTER THREE

# Emotional Blocks

This CHAPTER WILL BEGIN with a game—a game that requires a group of people, the larger the better, so try it at a party. It was, I think, invented by Bob McKim and is called "Barnyard."

**Exercise:** Divide your group and assign them to be various animals as follows:

| If their last names begin with: | they are: |
|---|---|
| A–E | sheep |
| F–K | pigs |
| L–R | cows |
| S–Z | turkeys |

Now tell each person to find a partner (preferably someone he or she does not know too well) and to look this partner in the eye. You will then count to three at which time everyone is to make the sound of the animal as loudly as they possibly can. See how loud a barnyard you can build.

The participants in this game will be able to experience a common emotional block to conceptualization—namely, that of feeling like an ass. If you did not play the game and want to experience the feeling, merely stand alone on any busy corner (or wherever you are right now) and loudly make the sound of one of the animals.

As we will see in the next chapter, conceptualization is risky and new ideas are hard to evaluate. The expression of a new idea, and especially the process of trying to convince someone else it has value, sometimes makes you feel like an ass, since you are doing something that possibly exposes your imperfections. In order to avoid this feeling, people will often avoid conceptualization, or at least avoid publicizing the output.

## The Mystery Of Emotion

Although emotions are central to problem solving, indeed to being human, many of us seem to be a bit uncomfortable in dealing with them. This is partly due to the mysterious nature of their mechanisms. If we do not understand things that happen within our mind, we tend to ignore them. As an example, we are quite comfortable with certain aspects of vision. The eye is a convenient analog to a camera (or vice versa) in that there is a lens, a diaphragm, and a layer of sensitive material (the retina) on which the image is captured. The optic nerve, which transmits this information to the brain, undoubtedly processing it a bit en route, is less well known, but we think of it as a bundle of wires. But the processing of visual information in the brain is so far from our intuition that we prefer to avoid thinking about it. Researchers have discovered some correlation between particular neurons and components of images, but they do not yet have a model that allows us to comfortably deal with the process that converts the electrical signals from our eye to our visual reality. Most people find it easier to assume the equivalent of what is sometimes called the homunculus, or little man sitting in the skull and watching a TV set displaying the image on the retina. Since we secretly know there is not one in there, we do not dwell on the mechanism.

In the case of emotions, we don't even have the satisfaction of the analog to the camera. We smell the ocean and fill with joy. We awaken depressed. We are terrified of speaking in public. We hate our boss. What is going on? For those of us who like to understand process, it is much easier to think about the perceptual blocks in the last chapter than emotional ones.

Part of the problem has to do with the complexity of the mechanisms. At the time of this writing there is a very popular book entitled *Emotional Intelligence* abroad in the land. It was written by Daniel Goleman, who was once editor of *Psychology Today* and later the cognitive science editor for the *New York Times*. The book is highly readable, summarizes research that attempts to explain various characteristics of emotion, and pleads for more consideration of emotion as an important aspect of personal success. When Goleman comes to listing emotions, he comes up with the following: anger, sadness, fear, enjoyment, love, surprise, disgust, and shame. But he then lists synonyms for each. As an example, under anger we find fury, outrage, resentment, wrath, exasperation, indignation, vexation, acrimony, animosity, annoyance, irritability, hostility, pathological hatred, and violence.

My students repeatedly come up with lists of emotions that differ from Goleman's and argue about the meanings of complementary descriptive words. Obviously, the complexity of emotions does not allow a simple model—at least one that can be made up of words in the English language. We can describe our sense of taste by saying it can distinguish sweet, sour, bitter, and salty. (Incidentally, that is all that taste can detect. The rest of the joy of food comes through smell.) We do not have anything that precise for emotions.

I have assigned Goleman's book to my students because it describes what researchers are discovering about mechanics of emotion and why they play such a powerful role in problem-solving. When I went to school, we were taught that the cortex analyzes signals from the senses and triggers appropriate responses. For instance, we are awakened at night by a strange sound in the house and our cognitive machinery analyzes what it might be. If the conclusion is that it is a prowler in the house, we become frightened. Present research indicates that signals from the senses go both to the cortex and to the amygdala and hippocampus. The latter two subsystems of the brain contain some basic memory of sensory signals that connote danger. We therefore begin being frightened before the cortex can analyze the data. The hypothalamus starts the flight-or-fight response, with the heart rate and blood pressure increasing, circulation increasing in large muscles and away from the gut and breathing slowing. The cingulate cortex tones the large muscles, freezes unrelated movements, and causes our face to assume a fearful expression. The locus ceruleus releases norepinephrine focusing our attention and prioritizing our knowledge and memories. This is all automatic. Later when the cortex reaches its conclusion, it may turn all of this off if the noise is simply the cat. Alternately it may reinforce the response. However, the important point to us is that emotions lead, not follow. This helps explain, for instance, why we often form such a strong first impression of a person, even though subsequent experience slowly teaches us that we were wrong. Also why emotions play such a strong role in conceptual thinking.

Unfortunately, scientific research tends to avoid emotion because of this complexity. Rigorous research demands that experiments be repeatable and that the results be measurable. Academic psychology in the first half of the twentieth century was dominated by behaviorists (Pavlov, Skinner) who considered behavior to be simply response to stimuli. They were not sure how to handle emotion. They did most of their experiments with animals such as rats, pigeons, cats, and dogs. If one runs a rat through a maze, does something to the rat, and then runs it through the maze again, one can quantitatively measure changes in its behavior and be somewhat confident of the ability to replicate the experiment. But how about using humans as experimental subjects? How do you keep your subjects from becoming annoyed with running the maze and going home? Imagine the loss in simplicity if one tries to do an experimental investigation of teenagers falling in love, or even an academic psychology department. Where is the repeatability? Where is the quantification? The cognitive psychologists who now dominate research have so far been hesitant to delve deeply into emotion. This may be a reason other than complexity why our models and our understanding of mechanisms seem so inadequate.

Because of its "fuzziness," psychological theory that deals more directly with emotion is often given the back seat by contemporary researchers. For instance, although they are alive and well in our culture and important viewpoints in therapy, the theories of Freud and his followers and of the humanistic psychologists (Rogers, Maslow, et al.) are not presently given the attention of cognitive and behavioral psychology in the field. They are worth mentioning here, however, because they do give importance to feelings, and because they have been prominent in many theories of creativity.

## Freud

Much of Freudian theory is based upon conflicts between the *id* (the instinctive animal part of ourselves) and the *ego* (the socially aware and conscious aspect) and *superego* (the moralistic portion of ourselves that forbids and prohibits). The motive force in the Freudian model is the id, which resides in the unconscious and is concerned with satisfying our needs. According to Freud, ideas originating in the unconscious must be subjected to the scrutiny of the ego (which may reject them because we cannot realistically carry them out) and the superego (which may reject them because we should not have let ourselves have such ideas in the first place). If these ideas are rejected, they will either be completely repressed or they will contribute to neurotic behavior because of unresolved conflict. If they are accepted, they will be admitted to the conscious mind. (This acceptance may be accompanied by anxiety, since once the ego and superego identify with an idea one can be hurt by its rejection.) If the ego and superego are overly selective, relatively few creative ideas will reach the conscious mind. If they are not selective enough, a torrent of highly innovative but extremely impractical ideas will emerge.

de Chirico, *The Anxious Journey*, 1913.

Since the time of Freud, his theory has been elaborated upon by his followers. A good example of this can be seen in Lawrence S. Kubie's book *Neurotic Distortion of the Creative Process*. Kubie utilizes the Freudian concept of *preconscious* in his model of creative thinking. He relegates the subconscious portions of creative thought and problem-solving to this preconscious, reserving the unconscious for unsettled conflicts and repressed impulses. In this model, the preconscious mental processes are hindered both by the conscious and the unconscious processes. As Kubie states in *Neurotic Distortion:*

> Preconscious processes are assailed from both sides. From one side they are nagged and prodded into rigid and distorted symbols by unconscious drives which are oriented away from reality and which consist of rigid compromise formations, lacking in fluid inventiveness. From the other side they are driven by literal conscious purpose, checked and corrected by conscious retrospective critique.

Like Freud, Kubie has a model of the mind in which creative thinking is inhibited by the conscious ego and superego and in which creativity occurs at least partly below the conscious level. However, neuroses play a much more villainous role in Kubie's model than in Freud's.

## The Humanistic Psychologists

Although humanistic psychologists agree that creativity is a response to basic inner needs in people, they have a somewhat broader hierarchy of needs than the Freudians. They maintain that people create in order to grow and to fulfill themselves, as well as to solve conflicts and to answer the cravings of the id. They are more concerned with reaching upward and outward. Carl Rogers, in an article entitled "Toward a Theory of Creativity" in *Creativity and its Cultivation* (edited by Harold Anderson) explains:

> The mainspring of creativity appears to be the same tendency which we discover so deeply as the curative force in psychotherapy—man's tendency to actualize himself, to become his potentialities. By this I mean the directional trend which is evident in all organic and human life— the urge to expand, extend, develop, mature—the tendency to express and activate all the capacities of the organism, to the extent that such activation enhances the organism or the self. This tendency may become deeply buried under layer after layer of encrusted psychological defenses; it may be hidden behind elaborate facades which deny its existence; it is my belief, however, based on my experience, that it exists in every individual and awaits only the proper conditions to be released and expressed.

The humanistic psychologists feel that the creative person is emotionally healthy and sensitive both to the needs and the capabilities of the unconscious to produce creative ideas. Like Freud's creative person, he or she possesses a strong ego and a realistic superego which allow prolific conceptualizing and relative freedom from distracting neuroses.

We can arrive at several interesting and believable conclusions, from the theories of Freudians and Humanists.

1. Humans create for reasons of inner drive, whether it be for purposes of conflict resolution, self-fulfillment, or both. They can, of course, also create for other reasons, such as money.
2. At least part of creativity occurs in a part of the mind which is below the conscious level.
3. Although creativity and neuroses may stem from the same source, creativity tends to flow best in the absence of neuroses.
4. The conscious mind, or ego, is a control valve on creativity.
5. Creativity can provoke anxieties.

What can we conclude about creativity from other fields of psychology? Our handling of the perceptual blocks discussed in the previous chapter can benefit from the insights of the cognitive psychologists. Better understanding of the brain's function can result in an improved ability to use it in new ways. Behaviorists tell us about the effect of reward and punishment and the social psychologists remind us of the powerful role of our friends, colleagues, and public opinion on our actions. We will be discussing such things more in Chapters 8 and 9. Neuro-physiologists and pharmacologists are learning about the importance of the physiological state of the brain and coming up with methods of altering brain behavior chemically (an approach to modifying creativity that is as yet highly controversial.)

Let us now turn to a few specific examples of emotional blocks so that we can become clearer on their causes and characteristics. These blocks may interfere with our ability to explore and manipulate ideas, with our ability to conceptualize fluently and flexibly—and prevent us from communicating ideas to others in a manner which will gain them acceptance. A few of them are:

1. Fear to make a mistake, to fail, to risk
2. Inability to tolerate ambiguity; overriding desires for security, order; "no appetite for chaos"
3. Preference for judging ideas, rather than generating them
4. Inability to relax, incubate, and "sleep on it"
5. Lack of challenge (problem fails to engage interest) versus excessive zeal (overmotivation to succeed quickly)
6. Inability to distinguish reality from fantasy

### Fear of Taking a Risk

Fear to make a mistake, to fail, or to take a risk is perhaps the most general and common emotional block. Most of us have grown up rewarded when we produce the "right" answer and punished if we make a mistake. When we fail we are made to realize that we have let others down (usually someone we love). Similarly we are taught to live safely (a bird in the hand is worth two in the bush, a penny saved is a penny earned) and avoid risk whenever possible. Obviously, when you produce and try to sell a creative idea you are taking a risk: of making a mistake, failing, making an ass of yourself, losing money, hurting yourself, or whatever.

This type of fear is to a certain extent realistic. Something new is usually a threat to the status quo, and is therefore resisted with appropriate pressure upon its creator. The risks involved with innovation often can result in real hardship. Far be it from me to suggest that people should not be realistic in assessing the costs of creativity. For instance, I spend a great amount of time attempting to explain to students that somehow the process of making money out of a commercially practical idea seems to require at least eight years, quite a bit of physical and emotional degradation, and often the sacrifice of such things as marriages and food. However, as I also try to explain to students, the fears that inhibit conceptualization are often *not* based upon a realistic assumption of the consequences. Certainly, a slightly "far-out" idea submitted as an answer to a class assignment is not going to result in loss of life, marriage, or even net worth. The only possible difficulty would arise if I, the teacher, were annoyed with the answer (and I happen to like such responses from students). The fear involved here is a more generalized fear of taking a chance.

One of the better ways of overcoming such a block is to realistically assess the possible negative consequences of an idea. As is sometimes asked, "What are your catastrophic expectations?" If you have an idea for a better bicycle lock and are considering quitting a job and founding a small business based upon the lock and a not-yet-conceived product line to go with it, the risks are considerable (unless you happen to have large sums of money and important commercial contacts). If you invent a new method of flight (say, wings of feathers held together with wax) the risks may also be considerable in perfecting the product. However, if you think of a new way to schedule your day, paint your bathroom, or relate to others in your dormitory, the risks are considerably less.

In my experience, people do not often realistically assess the probable consequences of a creative act. Either they blithely ignore any consequences, or their general fear of failure causes them to attach excessive importance to any "mistake," no matter how minor it will appear in the eyes of future historians. Often the potential negative consequences of exposing a creative idea can be easily endured. If you have an idea that seems risky, it is well worth the time to do a brief study of the possible consequences. During the study, you should include "catastrophic expectations" (assume everything goes badly) and look at the result. By doing this, it will become apparent whether you want to take the risk or not.

**Exercise:** Next time you are having difficulty deciding whether to push a "creative" idea, write a short (two-page) "catastrophic expectations" report. In it detail as well as you can precisely what would happen to you

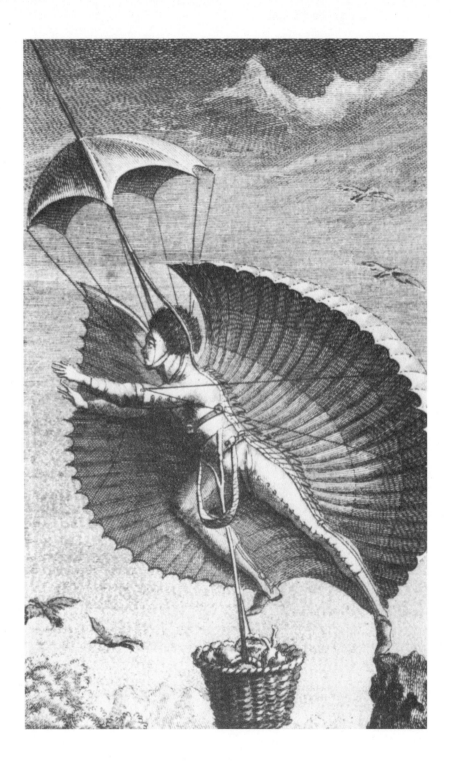

*if everything went wrong.* By making such information explicit and facing it, you swap your analytical capability for your fear of failure—a good trade.

## No Appetite for Chaos

The fear of making a mistake is, of course, rooted in insecurity, which most people suffer from to some extent. Such insecurities are also responsible for the next emotional block, the "Inability to tolerate ambiguity; overriding desire for order; 'no appetite for chaos.'" Once again, some element of this block is rational. I am not suggesting that in order to be creative you should shun order and live in a totally chaotic situation. I am talking more of an excessive fondness for order in all things. The solution of a complex problem is a messy process. Rigorous and logical techniques are often necessary, but not sufficient. You must usually wallow in misleading and ill-fitting data, hazy and difficult-to-test concepts, opinions, values, and other such untidy quantities. In a sense, problem-solving is *bringing order to chaos.* A desire for order is therefore necessary. However, the ability to tolerate chaos is a must.

We all know compulsive people, those who must have everything always in its place and who become quite upset if the order of their physical lives is violated. If this trait carries over into a person's mental process, he is severely impaired in his ability to work with certain types of problems. One reason for extreme ordering of the physical environment is efficiency. Another may be the aesthetic satisfaction of precise physical relationships. However, another reason is insecurity. If your underwear is precisely folded and "dressed right," you have precise control over your underwear, and thus there is one less thing out of control to be threatening. I do not actually care how your underwear is stored. However, if your thoughts are precisely folded and dressed right, you are probably a fairly limited problem-solver. The process of bringing widely disparate thoughts together cannot work too well because your mind is not going to allow widely disparate thoughts to coexist long enough to combine.

## Judging Rather than Generating Ideas

The next emotional block, the "Preference for judging ideas, rather than generating them," is also the "safe" way to go. Judgment, criticism, tough-mindedness, and practicality are of course essential in problem-solving. However, if applied too early or too indiscriminately in the problem-solving process, they are extremely detrimental to conceptualization. In problem-solving, analysis, judgment, and synthesis are three distinct types of thinking. In *analysis*, there is usually a right answer. I am an engineer: if you pay me to tell you how large a beam is needed to hold up a patio roof, you rightly expect *the* answer. Fortunately, I know how to analyze such things mathematically and can give it to you. *Judgment* is generally used in a problem where there are several answers and one must be chosen. A court case is a good example. Determining whether President Clinton broke the law is another. Judgments are made by sensible people as to guilt or innocence, and the situation is sufficiently complex that disagreements can occur. *Synthesis* is even more of a multianswer situation. A design problem (design a better way to serve ice cream) has an infinitude of answers, and there are few rigorous techniques to help in deciding between them.

If you analyze or judge too early in the problem-solving process, you will reject many ideas. This is detrimental for two reasons. First of all, newly formed ideas are fragile and imperfect—they need time to mature and acquire the detail needed to make them believable. Secondly, as we will discuss later, ideas often lead to other ideas. Many techniques of conceptualization, such as brainstorming, depend for their effectiveness on maintaining "way-out" ideas long enough to let them mature and spawn other more realistic ideas. It is sometimes difficult to hold onto such ideas because people generally do not want to be suspected of harboring impractical thoughts. However, in conceptualization one should not judge too quickly.

The judgment of ideas, unfortunately, is an extremely popular and rewarded pastime. One finds more newspaper space devoted to judgment (critic columns, political analyses, editorials, etc.) than to the *creation* of ideas. In the university, much scholarship is devoted to judgment, rather than creativity. One finds that people who heap negative criticism upon all ideas they encounter are often heralded for their practical sense and sophistication. Bad-mouthing everyone else's concepts is in fact a cheap way to attempt to demonstrate your own mental superiority.

If you are a professional idea-haver, your criticism tends to be somewhat more friendly. Professional designers are often much more receptive to the ideas of our students than non-design oriented faculty members. Professional problem-solvers have a working understanding of the difficulty in having ideas and a respect for ideas, even if they are flawed. If you are a compulsive idea-judger, you should realize that this is a habit that may exclude ideas from your own mind before they have had time to bear fruit. You are taking little risk (unless you are excluding ideas that could benefit you) and are perhaps feeding your ego somewhat with the thrill of being able to judge the outputs of others, but you are sacrificing some of your own creative potential.

### Inability Or Unwillingness to Incubate

Whether you believe that there is such a thing as unconscious thought or not, there is general agreement that answers to problems often suddenly appear in the mind, usually after thinking about the problem in some depth and often at strange times. One maddeningly familiar phenomenon to many people is a late answer to an important problem. You may work for days or weeks on a problem, complete it, and go on to other activities. Then, at some seemingly random point in time, a better answer "appears." Since the original problem was probably completed in order to reach a deadline, this "better" answer often only serves to annoy you that you did not think of it sooner. This better answer seems to result from an "incubation" process that was occurring in the mind. I have found in my own case that this "incubation" process works and is reliable. I have the confidence to think hard about a problem (charging up my unconscious) and then forget about it for a period of time. When I begin work on it again, new answers are usually present.

Many "symptoms" of incubation are common. There is a widespread belief among students that they do their best work just before deadlines. If, in fact, they work on the material when they receive it long enough to store the data in their unconscious, then incubation can occur, and a better solution may emerge at a later time. Incubation does often seem to produce the right answer at the appropriate time. Students often claim to have come up with a winning idea the morning that it is due, after struggling futilely with the problem for days.

You should allow the mind to struggle with problems over time. Incubation is important in problem-solving. It is poor planning not to allow adequate time for incubation in the solution of an important problem. It is also important to be able to relax in the midst of problem-solving. Your overall compulsiveness is less fanatical when you are relaxed, and the mind is more likely to deal with seemingly "silly" combinations of thoughts. If you are never relaxed, your mind is usually on guard against non-serious activities, with resulting difficulties in the type of thinking necessary for fluent and flexible conceptualization.

## Lack of Challenge versus Excessive Zeal

"Lack of challenge" and "excessive zeal" are opposite villains. You cannot do your best on a problem unless you are motivated. Professional problem-solvers learn to be motivated somewhat by money and future work that may come their way if they succeed. However, challenge must be present for at least some of the time, or the process ceases to be rewarding. On the other hand, an excessive motivation to succeed, especially to succeed quickly, can inhibit the creative process. The tortoise-and-the-hare phenomenon is often apparent in problem-solving. The person who thinks up the simple elegant solution, although he may take longer in doing so, often wins. As in the race, the tortoise depends upon an inconsistent performance from the rabbit. And if the rabbit spends so little time on conceptualization that he merely chooses the first answers that occur, such inconsistency is almost guaranteed.

### *Reality and Fantasy*

"Lack of access to areas of imagination," "Lack of imaginative control," and "Inability to distinguish reality from fantasy" will be discussed in more detail in Chapter Six. In brief, the imagination attempts to create objects and events. The creative person needs to be able to control his or her imagination and needs complete access to it. If all senses are not represented (not only sight, but also sound, smell, taste, and touch) the imagination cannot serve as well as it otherwise could. All senses need representation not only because problems involving all senses can be attacked, but also because imagery is more powerful if they are all called upon. If you think purely verbally, for instance, there will be little imagery available for the solving of problems concerning shapes and forms. If visual imagery is also present, the imagination will be much more useful, but still not as potent as if the other senses are also present. You can usually imagine a ball park much more vividly if you are able to recall the smell of the grass, the taste of the peanuts and beer, the feel of the seats and the sunshine, and the sounds of the crowd.

The creative person must be able not only to vividly form complete images, but also to manipulate them. Creativity requires the *manipulation* and *recombination* of experience. An imagination that cannot manipulate experience is limiting to the conceptualizer. You should be able to imagine a volcano being born in your ball park, or an airplane landing in it, or the ball park shrinking as the grass simultaneously turns purple, if you are to make maximum use of your imagination. Chapter Six will

contain some exercises to allow you to gauge your ability to control your imagination as well as discussions on how to strengthen the "mental muscle" used in imagining.

The creative person needs the ability to fantasize freely and vividly, yet must be able to distinguish reality from fantasy. If fantasies become too realistic, they may be less controllable. If you cannot go through the following exercise without a sense of acute physical discomfort, you may have difficulty distinguishing reality from fantasy. The exercise is taken from *Put Your Mother on the Ceiling* written some time ago by Richard de Mille. Stay with each fantasy (marked off by slashes) until you have it fully formed in your imagination. This game is called *breathing*.

Let us imagine that we have a goldfish in front of us. Have the fish swim around. / Have the fish swim into your mouth. / Take a deep breath and have the fish go down into your lungs, into your chest. / Have the fish swim around in there. / Let out your breath and have the fish swim out into the room again. /

Now breathe in a lot of tiny goldfish. / Have them swim around in your chest. / Breathe them all out again. /

Let's see what kind of things you can breathe in and out of your chest. / Breathe in a lot of rose petals. / Breathe them out again. / Breathe in a lot of water. / Have it gurgling in your chest. / Breathe it out again. / Breathe in a lot of dry leaves. / Have them blowing around in your chest. / Breathe them out again. / Breathe in a lot of raindrops. / Have them pattering in your chest. / Breathe them out again. / Breathe in a lot of sand. / Have it blowing around in your chest. / Breathe it out again. / Breathe in a lot of little firecrackers. / Have them all popping in your chest. / Breathe out the smoke and bits of them that are left. / Breathe in a lot of little lions. / Have them all roaring in your chest. / Breathe them out again. /

Breathe in some fire. / Have it burning and crackling in your chest. / Breathe it out again. / Breathe in some logs of wood. / Set fire to them in your chest. / Have them roaring as they burn up. / Breathe out the smoke and ashes. /

Have a big tree in front of you. / Breathe fire on the tree and burn it all up. / Have an old castle in front of you. / Breathe fire on the castle and have it fall down. / Have an ocean in front of you. / Breathe fire on the ocean and dry it up. /

What would you like to breathe in now? / All right. / Now what? / All right. / What would you like to burn up by breathing fire on it? / All right. /

Be a fish. / Be in the ocean. / Breathe the water of the ocean, in and out. / How do you like that? / Be a bird. / Be high in the air. / Breathe the cold air, in and out. / How do you like that? / Be a camel. / Be on the desert. / Breathe the hot wind of the desert, in and out. / How does that feel? / Be an old-fashioned steam locomotive. / Breathe out steam and smoke all over everything. / How is that? / Be a stone. / Don't breathe. / How do you like that? / Be a boy (girl). / Breathe the air of this room, in and out. How do you like that?

It would certainly be uncomfortable to inhale sand. Whether you can imagine the feeling of inhaling sand depends somewhat upon your ability to fantasize. No danger exists from imagining such an act, and any pain felt is imagined, not real. However, if your fantasies are confused with reality, it can be very difficult to fantasize such things. The imagination is extremely powerful because it can go beyond reality. But in order to do this, the imagination must be set free of the constraints placed upon *real* acts and events.

## Of Flow and Angst

Mihaly Cziksenthmihalyi is a professor of psychology at the University of Chicago who has interviewed a large number of creative people and concluded that when they at their most creative they are in a state he calls flow. In such a state they are completely consumed by their task. Time passes seemingly without notice and they are in a positive, perhaps even joyous emotional state. Most of us have experienced such times, sometimes at work, sometimes at play, when the process of creating something new is so captivating that it pushes our fears, cares, and worries aside. This state of flow is certainly something to be sought, since it is not only a fulfilling experience, but also consistent with the belief that negative emotions inhibit our creativity by influencing us toward the tried, true, and traditional. But we might ask about all of the famous creative people we hear about who have apparently lived fairly tortured lives, and how we attain this wonderful state.

Like most people, I have read the books and seen the movies about Van Gogh, Mozart, Oscar Wilde, Anne Sexton, and other highly creative people who apparently led traumatic and perhaps unhappy lives. But I do not personally know people in this category. This may be because I live a shallow life. It is also because I have not sought deeply disturbed people for friends and because I have spent my professional life in organizations which, like most organizations, are not comfortable in including them. If the portrait of Mozart in the movie *Amadeus* was accurate, he would have had trouble as a professor of music at Stanford. Similarly, the commonly held impression of Van Gogh would have been a bit much for the art department.

I believe that people at the edge of the norm can be and have been highly creative. A recent study concluded that outstanding painters are toward the ends of the psychological distribution. Another hypothesizes that those with bi-modal disease visualize in different ways than others. There are too many stories of eccentric-to-psychopathic geniuses to completely disbelieve them. However, my friends, colleagues, and past acquaintances include large numbers of people who are extremely successful in a wide variety of fields including the arts and who have won such things as Nobel, MacArthur, and Fielding Prizes, Oscars, Tonies, Presidential Medals, and memberships and achievement awards in a bewildering number of learned, honorary, and professional societies. Presumably they are creative. They are, as one would expect, unusually bright, curious, motivated, and sometimes lucky. However, they are disturbingly normal and not unusually tortured. They tend to interrupt their flow to worry about their kids, try to outwit the raccoons destroying their lawns, watch television, and wonder what they are going to do next in life.

Because of the directions my life has taken, my personal involvement with creativity has been in activities that take years to come to fruition, rather than days or hours. Technical projects cannot be done in a week. I have to teach a course a few times before I know how good/creative it is. Counting procrastination, it takes years for me to write a book. My friends with Nobel prizes and equivalent have spent years in education and in the field. Such time periods require reasonably stable people. They also say something about achieving flow.

During a creative activity, there are times of flow. How do we increase these times? Later in the book we will talk about motivation, but the short answer is that we are more likely to be creative if we love the things we are doing and we are more likely to spend time in the flow state. This is, of course, not an entirely useful answer. As an example, I am probably most in a state of flow (and perhaps most creative) when making things with my hands. Unfortunately, such activities do not seem to bring me other things I want in life. I seem to be fascinated by organizational politics and drawn to tilting windmills. I have therefore spent much time in jobs in which I have organizational responsibility—and which seem to involve hassle rather than flow. However, there are still times in such jobs when "everything is going just right" that have something to do with flow. And of course the rewards are great if one succeeds.

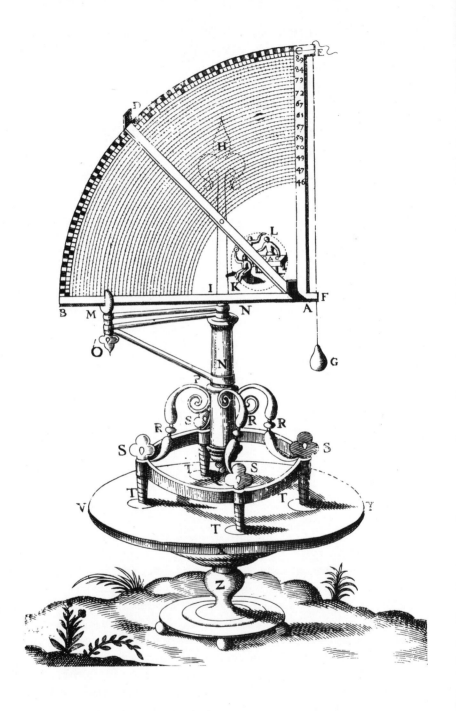

## CHAPTER FOUR

# Cultural and Environmental Blocks

WE ARE MEMBERS OF MANY CULTURES. There are not only national cultures, but cultures unique to regions within nations, religious beliefs, age, ethnicity, values, and other characteristics shared by a particular group of people. The trouble these groups have in understanding each other causes problems ranging from religious and racial wars through business failures to less than optimum vacation travel. Insensitivity to cultural factors inhibits creativity. Sensitivity can lead to unusual success in solving problems. Some examples of cultural blocks within the U.S. are:

1. Taboos
2. Fantasy and reflection are a waste of time, lazy, even crazy
3. Playfulness is for children only
4. Problem-solving is a serious business and humor is out of place
5. Reason, logic, numbers, utility, practicality are *good*; feeling, intuition, qualitative judgments, pleasure are *bad*
6. Any problem can be solved by scientific thinking and lots of money
7. Everyone should be like me
8. Cyber is better
9. Tradition is preferable to change

We also suffer from conceptual blocks due to the environment in which we solve problems. A few are:

1. Distractions—phone, easy intrusions
2. Lack of cooperation and trust among colleagues

3. Autocratic boss who values only his/her own ideas; does not reward others
4. Lack of support to bring ideas into action

Let us discuss cultural blocks first. We will begin by working a problem that will make the message clearer.

**Exercise:** Assume that a steel pipe is imbedded in the concrete floor of a bare room as shown below. The inside diameter is .06" larger than the diameter of a ping-pong ball (1.50") that is resting gently at the bottom of the pipe. You are one of a group of six people in the room, along with the following objects:

> 100' of clothesline
> A carpenter's hammer
> A chisel
> A box of Wheaties
> A file
> A wire coat hanger
> A monkey wrench
> A light bulb

List as many ways you can think of (in five minutes) to get the ball out of the pipe without damaging the ball, tube, or floor.

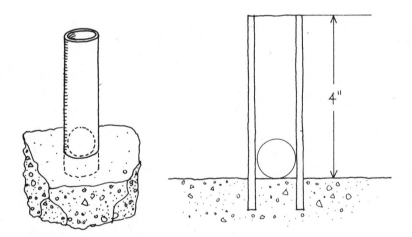

J. P. Guilford, who was a pioneer in the study of creativity, spoke a great deal about fluency and flexibility of thought. *Fluency* refers to the number of concepts one produces in a given length of time. If you are a fluent thinker, you have a long list of methods of retrieving the ball from the pipe. However, quantity is only part of the game. *Flexibility* refers to the diversity of the ideas generated. If you are a flexible thinker, you should have come up with a wide variety of methods. If you thought of filing the wire coat hanger in two, flattening the resulting ends, and making large tweezers to retrieve the ball, you came up with a solution to the problem, but a fairly common one. If you thought of smashing the handle of the hammer with the monkey wrench and using the resulting splinters to retrieve the ball, you were demonstrating a bit more flexibility of thought, since one does not usually think of using a tool as a source of splinters to do something with. If you managed to do something with the Wheaties, you are an even more flexible thinker.

Did you think of having your group urinate in the pipe? If you did not think of this, why not? The answer is probably a cultural block, in this case a *taboo*, since urinating is somewhat of a closet activity in the U.S.

## Taboos

I have used this ping-pong ball exercise with many groups and the response is not only a function of our culture, but also of the particular people in the group and the particular ambiance of the meeting. A mixed group newly convened in elegant surroundings will seldom think of urinating in the pipe. Even if members in the group do come up with this as a solution, they will keep very quiet about it. A group of people who work together, especially if all-male and if it's at the end of a working session, will instantly break into delighted chortles as they think of this and equally gross solutions. The importance of this answer is not that urinating in the pipe is necessarily the best of all solutions to the problem (although it is certainly a good one), but rather that cultural taboos can remove entire families of solutions from the ready grasp of the problem-solver. Taboos therefore are conceptual blocks. This is not a tirade against taboos. Taboos usually are directed against acts that would cause displeasure to certain members of a society. They therefore play a positive cultural role. However, it is the acts themselves which would offend. If imagined, rather than carried out, the acts are not harmful. Therefore, when working on problems within the privacy of your own mind, you do not have to be concerned with the violation of taboos.

If you want an example of the power of taboos, see if you can find a copy of a fascinating (and often out of print) book produced by the Cornell Architectural Department entitled *The Bathroom*. It is an analysis and critique of the western bathroom, and concludes that it is very poorly designed indeed. It is not altogether surprising to read that bathtubs are extremely dangerous as well as uncomfortable, and toilets neither do a good job of catching male urine streams nor place one in a good configuration for elimination. But the extent of material in the book makes one wonder why we stick with our traditional models. The answer, of course, is that bathing and elimination are slightly taboo topics in our culture. We do them in private and don't want to talk about them much. Urinals are obviously effective, but we do not want to make such a visible revolution in our home bathrooms. Bidets are useful, but most bathrooms do not contain them. Although this may be partly to save on floor space and plumbing, I think that it also reflects the reluctance of our society to admit to the need to apply water to genitalia.

Let us discuss a few more cultural blocks. The first two listed earlier, "Fantasy and reflection are a waste of time, lazy, even crazy" and "Playfulness is for children only," are challenged by quite a bit of evidence to indicate that fantasy, reflection, and mental playfulness are essential to good conceptualization. These are properties that seem to exist in children, and then unfortunately are to some extent socialized out of people in our culture. A four-year-old who amuses himself with an imaginary friend, with whom he shares his experiences and communicates, is cute. A 30-year-old with a similar imaginary friend is something else again.

(*LOCOMOTION.*)

"Daydreaming" or "woolgathering" is considered to be a symptom of an unproductive person.

As mentioned previously, environmental and cultural blocks are somewhat interrelated. People can fantasize much more easily in a supportive environment. We quite frequently ask students to fantasize as part of a design task, and when assigned the task they do quite well. However, they tend to feel quite guilty if they spend their time in fantasy if it is not an assigned part of the problem, since it often seems to be a diversion. Nevertheless, if you are attempting to solve a problem having to do with bickering children, is it not worth the time and effort to fantasize a situation in which your children do not bicker and proceed to examine the situation closely to see how it works? If you are designing a new recreational vehicle, should you not fantasize what it would be like to use that vehicle?

Many psychologists have concluded that children are more creative than adults. One explanation for this is that the adult is so much more aware of practical constraints. Another explanation, which I believe, is that our culture trains mental playfulness, fantasy, and reflectiveness out of people by placing more stress on the value of channeled mental activities. We spend more time attempting to derive a better world directly from what we have than in imagining a better world and what it would be. Both are important.

## Humor in Problem-Solving

Another cultural block mentioned was, "Problem-solving is a serious business and humor is out of place." Arthur Koestler was an important writer who among other topics, treated conceptualization. In an essay, "The Three Domains of Creativity," he identified these "domains" as *artistic originality* (which he called the "ah!" reaction), *scientific discovery* (the "aha!" reaction), and *comic inspiration* (the "haha!" reaction). He defined creative acts as *the combination of previously unrelated structures in such a way that you get more out of the emergent whole than you have put in.* He explained comic inspiration, for example, as stemming from "the interaction of two mutually exclusive associative contexts." As in creative artistic and scientific acts, two ideas have to be brought together that are not ordinarily combined. This is one of the essentials of creative thinking. In the particular case of humor, according to Koestler, the interaction causes us "to perceive the situation in two self-consistent but habitually incompatible frames of reference." The joke-teller typically starts a logical chain of events. The punch line then sharply cuts across the chain with a totally unexpected line. The tension developed in the first line is therefore shown to be a put-on and with its release, the audience laughs. Think of your favorite joke. Is Koestler's explanation of comic inspiration correct?

The critical point of interest here is that a similar reaction (laughter) may greet an original idea. A concept may be so contrary to the logical progress of the problem solution, precedent, or common intuition, that it may cause laughter. In fact any answer to a problem releases tension. Your unbelievably insightful solution to a problem may therefore be greeted with giggles and hoots, not only from others but even from yourself.

Creative groups in which I have worked have been funny. So are creative people I know. Humor is present in all sorts of ways and is important, because not only is it inseparable from new and original solutions, but decreases perception of risk. The emotional blocks discussed in the last chapter such as fear of failure are much less of a problem in a humorous atmosphere. Would you rather present a radical new idea to a group in good humor, or one that is coldly and completely analytical? I am not suggesting that creative activity is all fun, since it is fraught with frustration, detail work, and plain effort. However, humor is an essential ingredient of healthy conceptualization.

## Reason and Intuition

The fifth cultural block on our list is "Reason, logic, numbers, utility, practicality are *good;* feeling, intuition, qualitative judgement, pleasure are *bad.*" Reason, logic, numbers, utility, and practicality *are* good; but so, too, are feeling, intuition, qualitative judgment, and pleasure—especially if you are conceptualizing. This block against emotion, feeling, pleasure stems from our puritan heritage and our technology-based culture. It is extremely noticeable to me, since I work with large numbers of engineers and managers in situations where they must solve problems with a large amount of emotional content.

This block is particularly interesting because it has been affected by social changes that have occurred since I wrote the first edition of this book. Before the now-famous "late 60's," it was common to assign various mental activities and qualities by gender. It was thought that the female was sensitive, emotional, appreciative of the fine arts, and intuitive. The male was tough, physical, pragmatic, logical, and professionally productive. We now know that adhering to these constraints severely limited both sexes. Those interested in creativity knew it even then. Abraham Maslow described his findings about this block in his essay, "Emotional Blocks to Creativity" (found in *A Source Book for Creative Thinking*, edited by Parnes and Harding):

> One thing I haven't mentioned but have been interested in recently in my work with creative men (and uncreative men too) is the horrible fear of anything that the person himself would call "femininity," or "femaleness," which we immediately call "homosexual." If he's been brought up in a tough environment, "feminine" means practically everything that's creative. Imagination, fantasy, color, poetry, music, tenderness, languishing, and being romantic are walled off as dangerous to one's picture of one's own masculinity. Everything that's called "weak" tends to be repressed in the normal masculine adult adjustment. And many things are *called* weak which we are learning are not weak at all.

The opposite of this block also existed, of course. Many women were culturally conditioned to be as uncomfortable about many traits ascribed to the male (reason, logic, use of numbers, utility) as males are uncomfortable about "feminine" traits. Also, in the early 1970's when I wrote the first edition, the U.S. was in a wave in which the technological emphasis in our society was being blamed for many of man's difficulties. Those speaking out against this emphasis believed that feeling, intuition, and qualitative judgment are good and that reason, logic, numbers, utility, and practicality are not all that exciting.

In the late 1960's, the period in the U.S. sometimes known as the sexual revolution, gender roles came into question. By the early 1970's, intellectual stereotyping was much softer. Women were seeking and finding roles requiring toughness, quantitative thinking, and physical stamina and men were accepting that they could win through increased sensitivity and reliance upon intuition. Since then there has been continual experimentation and oscillation between "traditional" and "modern" roles. There is now some reversal of the "tough" woman and "sensitive" man. Various influential individuals, groups, and religions are seeking to re-establish older relationships between the sexes and there is much angst about resolving two-career families and child-rearing.

As far as creativity is concerned, the message is simple. Effective conceptualization requires the problem-solver to be able to incorporate all of these characteristics—the use of reason and logic, as well as intuition and feeling. The designer of physical things must be aesthetically sensitive if the quality of our world is going to improve, whether the designer happens to be male or female. Similarly, the designer must be able to view technology honestly and without disciplinary bias whether from an art background or an engineering background. The business-man must use intuition and the social scientist must use mathematics. The man must be sensitive and the woman strong.

### Left-Handed and Right-Handed Thinking

In reading the literature associated with conceptualization, one often encounters references to "left- and right-handed thinking." This is dis-cussed particularly well by Jerome Bruner in his book, *On Knowing: Essays for the Left Hand.* The right hand has traditionally been linked with law, order, reason, logic, and mathematics—the left with beauty, sensitivity, playfulness, feeling, openness, subjectivity, and imagery. The right hand has been symbolic of tools, disciplines, and achievement—the left with imagination, intuition, and subconscious thinking. In Bruner's words:

> . . . the one the doer, the other the dreamer. The right is order and law-fulness, *le droit.* Its beauties are those of geometry and taut implication. Reaching for knowledge with the right hand is science. . . . Of the left hand we say that it is awkward. . . . The French speak of the illegitimate descendant as being *à main gauche*, and though the heart is virtually at the center of the thoracic cavity, we listen for it on the left. Sentiment, intuition, bastardy. And should we say that reaching for knowledge with the left hand is art?

Oddly enough, this historical symbolic alignment of the two hands with two distinct types of thinking is consistent with present under-standing of brain function. The left hemisphere of the brain (which con-trols the right hand) contains the areas which are associated with con-trol of speech and hearing and involved with analytical tasks such as solving an algebra problem. The right hemisphere (which controls the left hand) governs spatial perception, synthesis of ideas, and aesthetic appreciation of art or music. However, this coincidence is not the main message here, which is that the effective conceptualizer must be able to utilize both right-handed and left-handed thinking. C. P. Snow, in his famous book hypothesizing the existence of two cultures, *Two Cultures and the Scientific Revolution*, separates scientists from humanists. Yet, if one *can* separate people that clearly, then the people one has separated are not maximizing their creative potential. The scientists who are responsible for breakthroughs in knowledge cannot operate entirely by extrapolating past work, but must utilize intuition, too. Similarly, the humanists who disregard the logical are doomed to be ineffectual (even counterproductive) in influencing social actions.

An emphasis on either type of thinking—to the disregard of the other—is a cultural block. In the professional world in our culture, the emphasis is placed on right-handed thinking. It is easier to get money to support right-handed thinking than left-handed thinking. More fathers want their sons to be lawyers, doctors, or scientists than painters, poets, or musicians. Until the culture is willing to accept the equal importance of left- and right-handed thinking in both sexes, a large number of its members will continue to suffer from this conceptual block.

> **Exercise:** Put yourself into a left-handed thinking mode. Stay away from logic, order, mathematics, science. Think about your feelings, beauty, sadness, the inputs that are coming to your senses. You can probably do this better by placing yourself in a conducive environment (under a tree in the springtime, alone in your most comfortable chair). Then switch yourself into a right-handed mode by thinking of a detailed plan to make money out of one of your left-handed thoughts. Are you ambidextrous? Are you able to shift from one type of thinking to the other, and ideally to do both at once? Or are you more comfortable with one type of thinking than the other?

The block entitled "Any problem can be solved by scientific thinking and lots of money" is of course a cultural one related to the emphasis on the importance of right-handed thinking. It is also interesting, because it exists partly as a result of popular misconception about the scientific process. Science depends both upon logical controlled progress (right-handed) and breakthroughs (often somewhat left-handed). Maslow, in his essay, "Emotional Blocks to Creativity," discusses primary creativity, which he describes as the "creativeness which comes out of the unconscious, and which is the source of new discovery (or real novelty) of ideas which depart from what exists at this point." This is the force behind the breakthroughs so necessary to science. He continues by speaking of what he calls secondary creativity, which he explains as follows:

> I am used now to thinking of two kinds of science, and two kinds of technology. Science can be defined, if you want to, as a technique whereby uncreative people can create and discover, by working along with a lot of other people, by standing upon the shoulders of people who have

come before them, by being cautious and careful, and so on. That I'll call secondary creativeness and secondary science.

## Primary and Secondary Creativity

The present awesome progress in genetics and biochemistry (through a large amount of secondary creativity) rests upon the discovery of RNA and DNA and their functions and structures (primary creativity). For a good treatment of this, read James P. Watson's *The Double Helix*, if you have not already. This is an intriguing book which talks about science in a way that is so contrary to many people's concept of the scientific method that it was very controversial when it first came out. It treats the discovery of the structure of DNA as a very human and very left-handed process. Watson and co-discoverer Francis Crick relied heavily on inspiration, iteration, and visualization. Even though they were superb biochemists, they had no precedent from which they could logically derive their structure and therefore relied heavily on left-handed thinking. The U.S. space effort during the 1960s was extremely impressive and exemplified the power of science—and technology based on science. However, a great deal of primary creativity and left-handed thinking was involved. Even such basic "scientific" decisions as whether to carry instruments to measure physical quantities or television cameras on the first lunar spacecraft were made in a left-handed way, since there was simply no way to make them with sheer logic. The design of the first spacecraft required a high degree of "art" (backed up, of course, by a great deal of analysis, detail design, and sophisticated fabrication and development) because there was no precedent that the designers could logically extend.

If "scientific thinking" is properly defined, it is extremely powerful for large-scale well-funded attacks on problems; however, right-handed science is only effective if based on established understanding. Right-handed science and lots of money can solve only problems that are solely in the domain of understood phenomena (a relatively small domain). Problems with social and emotional content and high complexity, such as crime in the cities, require a great deal more than right-handed science or secondary creativity.

Unfortunately, left-handed thinking and primary creativity are harder to explain, more difficult to predict, and less consistent than right-handed thinking and secondary creativity. It is therefore more difficult to write proposals that will bring support for such activities. It is easier for me to secure funding to work on the application of some newly discovered scientific phenomena (even though the potential good of the application may be small) than it is to find support for looking for a breakthrough. In the first case, the funding agency and I can be quite confident of the detailed nature of the work that needs to be done, the approximate amount of money needed, the schedule, and that I will in fact come up with something. In the second, there is no such security. The funding agency must judge me on the basis of intangibles such as my previous performance, my motivations, and my knowledge. The second is more of a gamble than the first. Support for science therefore also tends to be biased toward right-handed thinking, since most agencies handing out money must answer to someone and therefore tend to be somewhat conservative.

The "vagueness" of primary creativity and left-handed thinking, of course, also plagues those involved in the humanities and the soft sciences. Many of the soft sciences have sought to become more quantitative and rigorous in order to take better advantage of our cultural bias toward right-handed thinking. It is debatable whether this has been advantageous. Although a scientist, I am very sympathetic to the wails of those in the humanities and social sciences as to the lack of monetary support they receive from our society. At one point in my education (after I had become an engineer) I was enrolled in art school. A painting teacher I knew would from time to time tell me that I had an excellent background for painting. His reasoning was economic. He believed that many painters were hampered in the beginning of their careers by the necessity of holding down low-paying and long-houred jobs in order to support their families. He figured that I should be able to support myself by doing engineering work part-time and would therefore have time and energy available to paint. A strange observation, but perhaps a true one. It is much easier for me to find support for my lifestyle than it is for friends of mine who want to write or paint. The humanities and the social sciences are extremely vital in a mature society such as ours. Their importance is presently obscured by a massive cultural block.

## Everybody Should Be Just Like Me

People have different value systems and desires. They tend to reinforce this by associating with others with similar ones. Humans are quite tribal in this way and large collections of people, like a nation, consist of a large number of groups who disagree—liberals and conservatives, Catholics and Protestants, the wealthy and the poor, Bloods and Crips, the Hatfields and the McCoys. These interest groups tend to become more extreme in opposition to others. We therefore have the "far right" and the "radical left," the "Neo Christian Movement" and those who believe that God is dead, and various groups that become so frustrated that they adopt terrorist tactics.

The inability to see other people's viewpoints results not only in premature judgment, but in instantaneous opposition. As an academic, I am classified as a liberal and since I consult with technology-based businesses, often am in discussion with people who are highly conservative in their views. Although I may be getting paranoid, I sometimes think people are hostile to my technical opinions simply because of their stereotyping about professors. I know that engineering professors often devalue opinions of people from industry who are hostile to the academic life. Creativity can often result from the tension between the values and desires of different groups, but openness and acceptance are needed. To be convinced that all people who own guns are wrong, that abortion should be outlawed, that government should be abolished, or that the free market can solve all social problems pretty much guarantees that one will not contribute much creativity to problems having to do with gun deaths, unwanted pregnancies, national organization, or social welfare. To love information technology and to believe that eventually manual labor will be obsolete will not help one work with people who are not particularly interested in information. To believe that one has the right answer to complicated problems that have previously been worked on by large numbers of bright and motivated people (health care, international relations, the economy) is a normal response, but restricts one's creativity by closing one off to the thinking of the others.

## Cyber Is Better

There is an interesting version of this among those who crave a world in which everyone is electronically interconnected in a way so that they can not only communicate but also have access to great amounts of information and computational ability. This is the so-called "cyber" world. Unfortunately, not everyone is going to want to be interconnected to everyone and spend their hours digesting and manipulating information. Many people who are in love with digital devices believe that this is a temporary situation and eventually everyone will come to love the cyber world. This may be true as far as entertainment is concerned, but I think not universally. In her graduate work at Stanford, one of our students, Adria Anuzis Brown, came to some interesting conclusions during her research, which was a study of interaction between a U.S. and a Japanese company cooperating on the development of a product. She looked at three aspects of communication, which she called personal (same location, personal interaction), cultural (commonalties of interest, background, and values), and cyber (interacting electronically). She found that the most successful professional interaction made use of all three. Electronic interaction alone was not as successful as all three. In other words, the best creative work comes from people who are not only electronically interconnected, but also share cultural values and interact personally in the same physical space. Companies assuming that everyone will live in cyberspace will do fine as long as they are content with a customer base of like-minded people. If they want to go beyond that, they must become appreciative of the values of people like me, who have no interest at all in receiving more advertising messages or carrying G.P.S. receivers and cell-phones while backpacking.

## Tradition and Change

As a final, subtle cultural block, I would like to discuss briefly the concept: "Tradition is preferable to change." In his book *Notes on the Synthesis of Form*, Christopher Alexander discusses two types of culture, one that he calls the unselfconscious culture, and one the self-conscious culture. The unselfconscious culture is tradition oriented. Traditional form and ceremonies are perpetuated, and often taboos and legends work against change. The architect in such a culture would probably serve a long apprenticeship and learn how to make the traditional buildings (the long house, the temple). When he reached a stage in which he was judged competent by his elders, he would presumably become a master and train other apprentices. The United States is hardly such a culture. Any young architect knows better than to study traditional building forms. Ours is a self-conscious culture. New religions, forms, social movements, and styles in dress, talk, entertainment, and living crop up continually. Age and experience are venerated only if "relevant," and long apprenticeships are rapidly becoming extinct. A very high value seems to be placed on innovation.

Yet, strangely enough, many individuals value tradition more than they do change. This is probably good, since in my opinion our culture has little enough tradition. However, as far as good conceptualization is concerned, such an attitude has negative effects. Motivation is essential to creativity. No matter how talented the problem-solver, frustration and detail work are inescapable in problem-solving. Unless you truly *want* to solve a problem (for pleasure, money, prestige, comfort, or whatever) you probably will not do a very good job. Unless you are convinced that change is needed in a particular area, you are not likely to hypothesize ways of accomplishing that change.

The problem arises when individuals become so universally in favor of tradition that they cannot see the need for and desirability of change in specific areas. The true conservative, I suppose, would fall in this category. Some environmentalists lose their credibility by being totally against change in an area. If a person is truly grounded in the "good old days," and feels strongly that changes in the past 20 or 30 years have diminished rather than enhanced the quality of life, he is unlikely to be *motivated* to be a very good conceptualizer. He is culturally blocked. The person who is in favor of change for change's sake may be a more dangerous animal to have around. Yet, as far as conceptualization (the subject of this book) is concerned, he is probably in fairly good shape.

## Thinking Through Blocks

Projects requiring one to think through cultural blocks are among the most popular with our students, since the blocks are so difficult to overcome and yet so obvious once they have been overcome. We often ask our students to design puzzles, games, or situations for each other that require breaking through a cultural block in order to reach a solution. One project that sticks in my mind required that a dollar bill be removed from beneath a precariously balanced object without tipping over the object. This was extremely easy to do if the bill were torn in half. However, for various cultural reasons (it's illegal to deface money, one doesn't usually tear up things of value), no one thought of this particular solution, with the result that no one could remove the dollar. Another project required that one playing card out of a deck of 52 be destroyed. Once again no one thought of perpetrating such a crime (we are a society of card players and most of us do not approve of incomplete decks of cards). Still a third I can remember was perhaps the most basic I have seen. The solution of the problem required that a number of objects be moved around a board in a prearranged sequence in order to reach the desired final configuration. It turned out to be impossible to follow the rules and solve the problem. The cultural block? Following rules! It was simple to attain the desired configuration if the rules were violated.

A less flippant situation occurs when students from more rigid and theory-oriented disciplines take courses in design. Expertise in design is somewhat different from expertise in, say, fluid mechanics. Design is a multi-answer situation and analysis is used to gain an end, not for its own sake. The teacher, although hopefully experienced in the design process and in command of the necessary techniques, is not the usual type of academic expert, in that he or she does not have a monopoly on the "right" answers at the beginning of the course, and in fact may not even always come up with the "best" answer. Grading becomes much more subjective and the student must take more academic risk, since the evaluation standards are less orthodox. Students from a school system in which grading is extremely important, and in which the professor or teacher is an extreme authority figure, sometimes have difficulty in adapting to design courses. They are often preoccupied with "What is the answer?" and "How do I ensure that I will get an A?"—as well they should be, since their background has been exclusively oriented in such directions. The tragedy is that many foreign students from countries that need capable designers and problem-solvers suffer from such blocks. Academic risk-taking is somewhat of a taboo. Another culturally-induced difference between students from the U.S. and those from less industrially developed countries is the difference in their knowledge of, and attitude toward, machines. Students from the U.S., Western Europe, etc. have grown up with cars, motorcycles, and other such devices and are quite at home with them. Students from less industrially developed countries often have had less opportunity in their cultures to be exposed to machinery and are therefore somewhat less experienced and more inhibited in working with it.

## Environmental Blocks

Let us now move on to environmental blocks. These are blocks that are imposed by our immediate social and physical environment. The most obvious blocks are the physical. Plainly the physical surroundings of the problem-solver influence his productivity. I am sure that all of you are familiar with the effect of distractions. It is very difficult to work on complicated problems with continual phone interruptions. At times even potential distractions are a problem since when you are in a frustrating phase of problem-solving, you are quite tempted to take advantage of such opportunities. Personally speaking, when involved in problem-solving I will go to heroic efforts to be distracted. Often I have to force myself out of bed at an inhuman hour in the morning to work on a problem when I am sure I can find no alternative activities available and no one to talk to. Even then, I often just sit hoping that someone will wake up and distract me.

In fact my wife loves it when I write books. The bad news is my increased grouchiness. Like many (most?) people who write, I love to have written books, but the process of writing them verges between taxing and torturous. The good news is that I escape by painting the house, sanding the floors, repairing the roof, improving the garden irrigation, and doing other worthwhile things that I ordinarily keep in my procrastination folder. I am not among the extreme, however. One of my professor friends, who has a very nice office at the University and workspace in his home, was having little success in writing a book. He finally rented space in an office building in town, in which he put only material necessary to write his book—no phone, no extraneous books, no modem. He then paid the receptionist in the neighboring office to prevent him from leaving his office during the times he wanted to write. It worked!

The physical environment affects everyone. Yet, because of the individual habit patterns we all acquire, different individuals are affected differently. With regard to mental activity, some people work better in cold rooms, some in warm rooms, some in cold rooms with their feet wrapped in something warm. Some people work better to music and some in silence; some around others and some in isolation; some in windowless rooms and some in rooms with windows. Some are impervious to their visual surroundings and others are very sensitive to them.

## Supportive Environments

In his book, *The Art and Science of Creativity*, George Kneller discusses some of the sometimes bizarre devices many writers have adopted with respect to their working environment: "Schiller, for example, filled his desk with rotten apples; Proust worked in a cork-lined room; Mozart took exercise; Dr. Johnson surrounded himself with a purring cat, orange peel, and tea; Hart Crane played jazz loud on a Victrola. All these are aids to the intense concentration required in creative thinking. An extreme case is Kant, who would work in bed at certain times of the day with the blankets arranged round him in a way he had invented himself. While writing *The Critique of Pure Reason* he would concentrate on a tower visible from his window. When some trees grew up to hide the tower, he became frustrated, and the authorities of Königsberg cut down the trees so that he could continue his work."

Some people may have a particular environment in which they are most effective at conceptual work of any kind. Therefore we sometimes find the all-purpose studio, in which a person may paint, write, sculpt, invent, and whatever. Another person may have one environment in which he can best write, another in which he can best throw pots, and still a third in which he does woodworking. Even though such individual differences exist, we can still say that most individuals do conceptual work best in a particular type of environment.

**Exercise:** Take a piece of paper and list the characteristics of the most supportive possible environment you can think of for your own conceptual work (or different types of environment for different types of work). Do the environments in which you work resemble this? If not, why not? Assuming your hypothesized environment is practical for you (not the beaches of an as yet undiscovered South Sea island), change your working environment to more closely resemble your hypothetical one. Does this make an appreciable difference on your conceptual productivity?

Although environment usually has physical connotations, the most important environmental blocks are often not physical. In fact, if anything they verge on the cultural and on the emotional. As discussed in the last chapter, conceptualization involves a certain amount of emotional risk. Change is often threatening; therefore, so are new ideas. They can be quickly squelched, especially when newly born, imperfect, and not reduced to practice. The usual response of society, in fact, *is* to squelch such ideas. There are many ways to do this. One is to over-analyze them. Another is to laugh at them. Still another is to ignore them.

**Exercise:** Think up a new idea, maybe an invention, that sounds reasonably plausible. Maybe an electric toilet brush, or a mail campaign to convince the post office to improve its service, or anything else. Then seriously propose this idea to friends and (if you are brave) others you meet from time to time. Note their reactions. Are any, other than your friends, enthusiastic? (Are even your friends really receptive, or are they merely being polite?) This is a poor experiment since some of your ideas may be brilliant and some terrible, and this conceivably could influence the response. However, I do not think that the difference in response will be that large. If you want to improve the experiment, try both a brilliant and a poor idea on the same people.

## Accepting and Incorporating Criticism

Non-supportive responses are especially harmful when they come from bosses, colleagues, or friends. In Chapter Eight and Nine, we will discuss conceptualization in groups and in organizations. However, a few comments are in order here. An atmosphere of honesty, trust, and support is absolutely necessary if most people are to make the best of their conceptual abilities. There are exceptions, it is true. Many of the outstanding inventors I have known have been quite confident of their abilities and less dependent on support from others. One of the best of these idea-havers worked with me at one time. Given a problem he would instantly throw together a solution. These solutions were often so poorly thought out that I would almost break out in a rash. He would then happily go to the next office and receive enough criticism on the idea to send me into a depression for several days. He would then incorporate the criticism into his idea and proceed to the next office. In this way, he would literally construct a solution and usually an outstanding one. He was successful because of his ability to accept and incorporate criticism. However, people like this are rare.

Most people are not happy with criticism and, to make matters worse, are somewhat unsure of the quality of their own ideas. They therefore require a supportive environment in which to work. One of our most serious problems with students in design classes is that they hesitate to expose ideas about which they are unsure, not only to the faculty, but also to each other. Since many of their creative ideas fall into this not-sure category (naturally, since they have little else to judge these ideas by) they hesitate to reveal them. We have to convert the class (usually a listening, competitive, no-risk situation) into a friendly, noncompetitive, interactive situation in which people will take the risk of exposing their most impractical ideas to each other. Competition and lack of trust destroy such a supportive environment. No one likes to expose his magnificent concept if someone is going to steal it or be jealous.

## Autocratic Bosses

Bosses with answers are a particular problem in the engineering profession. Many productive problem-solvers are strong-headed. They can carry a concept through to completion in spite of apathy or hostility from others and the difficulty of finding support for a new idea. If they happen to have good judgment, they are able to accomplish noticeable achievements in a company environment and are often promoted in management. One therefore often finds that many managers are successful idea-havers who are stubborn enough to push their ideas through to completion. They tend to continue in this mode when managing others. Although a manager such as this can be an effective problem-solver, he is essentially operating with his own conceptual ability and an in-house service organization—he is probably not going to make much use of the conceptual ability of his subordinates. In order to maximize the creative output of a group, a manager must be willing and able to encourage his subordinates to think conceptually and to reward them when they succeed. He should, of course, conceptualize on his own. But he should do it somewhat in tandem with the other members of his group, if he is attempting to use them to their fullest. This is an obvious piece of advice that is surprisingly often ignored. Time and time again I have seen design groups operating mainly on the concepts of the group leader. Such a group admittedly can be successful if the leader is an outstanding conceptualizer and the members of the group are content to develop his ideas. However, our concern is with environmental blocks, and such a working situation is hardly an environment conducive to conceptualization on the part of the group members.

## Non-Support

Lack of physical, economic, or organizational support to bring ideas into action is also another common problem. New ideas are typically hard to bring into action. A great amount of effort is involved in perfecting an idea and then selling it. Many conceptual breakthroughs in science, for instance, have taken years of work to validate to the point where they would elicit interest from others in the scientific community. A novel itself is far removed from the original thought that inspired it. Even after the idea is fleshed out into a believable and complete form, it must be sold to an often skeptical world. This may require money and time. Again, using the inventor as an example: the small inventor is at a distinct disadvantage compared to the corporate inventor because of the fabrication needed, the test equipment desired, the legal and promotional expertise required, and the food and rent consumed while he or she is doing the inventing. Even the best of ideas is doomed if time and money are not available to push it to fruition.

Granted, the inventor is perhaps an extreme example. Nonetheless, even a concept for a new recipe is useless without the money to buy the ingredients and the time to cook it. A concept for a painting or a drawing is similarly useless without the supplies and the time. A concept for improving a marriage (take a vacation) requires economic and temporal support. All ideas require an environment that will produce the support necessary to bring them to fruition. This support may come from your friendly venture-capital firm, your bank, your spouse, your income surplus, or any other form of patronage. Lack of such patronage is a very effective environmental block.

VUE from SPOHRPLATZ à - FRIEDRICHSPLATZ - "Documenta". Christo 1967
Projet pour MONUMENTAL EMPAQUETAGE pour DOCUMENTA 1968
(THE TOP INFLATABLE PACKAGE floating with HELIUM)

## CHAPTER FIVE

# Intellectual and Expressive Blocks

INTELLECTUAL BLOCKS RESULT in an inefficient choice of mental tactics or a shortage of intellectual ammunition. Expressive blocks inhibit your vital ability to communicate ideas—not only to others, but to yourself as well. Let us look at the following blocks:

1. Solving the problem using an incorrect language (verbal, mathematical, visual)—as in trying to solve a problem mathematically when it can more easily be accomplished visually
2. Inflexible or inadequate use of intellectual problem-solving strategies
3. Lack of, or incorrect, information
4. Inadequate language skill to express and record ideas (verbally, musically, visually, etc.).

A few examples should help us understand these blocks better. The monk puzzle described in the first chapter of this book is one in which choosing the correct language (visual) leads you rapidly toward a solution. Here is another "language" problem:

**Exercise:** Picture a large piece of paper, the thickness of this page. In your imagination, fold it once (now having two layers), fold it once more (now having four layers), and continue folding it over upon itself 50 times. How thick is the 50-times-folded paper?

It is true that it is impossible to fold any piece of paper, no matter how big or how thick, 50 times. But for the sake of the problem, imagine that you can. When you either have the answer or have given up, continue.

Your *first fold* would result in a stack 2 times the original thickness. Your *second* would give you a stack $2 \times 2$ times the original thickness.

Your *third:* $2 \times 2 \times 2$ times the original thickness. Extending this, if you are somewhat of a mathematician, you should recognize that the answer to the problem is $2^{50}$ times the original thickness ($2^{50}$ happens to be about 1,100,000,000,000,000). If the paper is originally the thickness of typing paper, the answer is some 50,000,000 miles or over half the distance from the earth to the sun.

If you tried to attack this particular problem with visual imagery (the clever way to handle the monk puzzle) you probably could not get an answer, since it is next to impossible to accurately visualize 50 folds. If you attacked it verbally, you probably also had trouble. If you are familiar with doubling problems, you knew that the answer was a surprisingly big number, but still could not place a value on it. The correct language in this problem was clearly mathematics.

## Choosing Your Problem-Solving Language

Once again, how did you select the mental strategy you used to work on this problem? How did you decide to use visualization, mathematics, or whatever? If you were faked into visualization by our mention of the monk problem, you chose it consciously. If you are really getting the message of this book, you consciously thought about various ways of working the problem and then picked one. However, many of you probably once again *unconsciously* selected a strategy and then unconsciously switched from one strategy to the other. As we said before, most people follow this *habit* pattern in problem-solving. Without conscious thought, a direction will occur in the mind. This direction may or may not be the right one. If it is a wrong one, another may or may not appear.

It is possible to aid this strategy selection by consciously considering the various languages of thought you might use. For instance, you could have read the paper folding problem and then said to yourself, "Let's see, this guy has been trying to sell me visual thinking. Can I solve it visually? I'll try a few folds. [Task becomes difficult.] What else could I try? Verbalization? Probably not—since it is a physical problem asking for quantitative data. Hey, quantitative—how about mathematics?" At this point, you either solve it by inspection (you're a pro), write out equations and solve them (semi-pro) or ask someone you know who knows math (amateur).

Here is another puzzle. Before you try thinking of the answer, examine the problem and see what mental languages seem appropriate. Then attack the problem in the most appropriate language:

**Exercise:** A man and a woman standing side by side begin walking so that their right feet hit the ground at the same time. The woman takes three steps for each two steps of the man. How many steps does the man take before their left feet simultaneously reach the ground?

This is a good problem to solve with visual thinking. A live experiment with another person, a drawing, or a musical rhythm analogy will all work well. A mathematical approach will work, although it is somewhat circuitous. Verbalization, once again, will not get you very far. What language did you pick? Did it work? Did you try alternate approaches? How did you know it was time to give up on one and try another? The answer is that their left feet never hit the ground simultaneously.

Choice of the proper problem-solving language is difficult not only because the choice is usually made unconsciously, but also because of the heavy emphasis on verbal thinking (with mathematical thinking a poor second) in our culture. The two problems you just worked were difficult because neither can be easily solved by the application of verbal thinking. Visualization, as expressed through the use of drawings, is almost essential in designing physical things well. One reason for this is that verbal thinking, when applied to the design of physical things, has the strange attribute of allowing you to think that you have an answer when, in fact, you do not. Verbal thinking among articulate persons is fraught with glib generalities. And in design it is not until one backs it up with the visual mode that one can see whether one is fooling oneself or not.

Now that you are sensitized to this situation, let me give you an exercise that will give you some insight to your own biases. It subjects you to three types of problem solving: verbal-expressive, visual-design, and mathematical. As in past exercises, try to remain aware of how you respond to the three parts of the exercise both cognitively (thinking) and emotionally.

Find a few friends to do this with. It will make the differences in specialization more apparent. The exercise takes about twenty minutes. If you have a representative group of friends, everyone will feel somewhat uncomfortable during at least one of the five-minute exercises. Some of you may not like any of them. All three of the activities you will do require creativity, are of high status, and earn people fame and money. However, to the extent that you feel uncomfortable doing one of them, you probably avoid such activities and do not communicate too well with those who enjoy them. We tend to stay within our habits, with an accompanying loss of creativity.

**Exercise:**
1. Spend five minutes writing a short and serious poem on love. strive for beauty and expression. At the end of five minutes, read your poems to each other.
2. Spend five minutes designing (graphically—draw it on paper) a better desk lamp. Desk lamps usually have shortcomings, whether functional or aesthetic. Draw one that is both functionally successful and beautiful. At the end of the time, show your design to the others in the group and discuss it for a few minutes.
3. Spend five minutes working on the following problem: an ant is in a top corner of a square room that measures 24 ft on a side and is 8 ft high. He sees an edible crumb at the opposite bottom corner. The ant wants to walk to the crumb over the shortest possible path. How long is the path? After the five minutes are over, make sure that everyone in the group understands and agrees upon the answer.

Our reaction to intellectual problems does not necessarily reflect our present ability to solve them. We have all manner of outdated measures and anxieties that influence us. I often give the poetry portion of the exercise to engineering and business students, professional engineers and managers, and business executives. The initial response of the group to the assignment typically runs the gamut from horror to an urgent need to leave the room. However, as the participants begin working on their poems, they find that the process is less painful than they might have thought. They have long-dormant habits remaining from previous schooling with which to construct poetic forms. They also find that they have a lot to say about love, although it may not be information that is consistent with their usual communication habits. The pain returns, however, when they have to divulge their poems to others. After they have read their poems to each other, I usually find that if I ask those whose poems were terrible to raise their hands, all hands are raised. If I then ask the same of those who heard a poem that was surprisingly good, all hands will again be raised. In other words, they all think their own poems are terrible but that those written by the other people are pretty good.

I have occasionally asked Diane Middlebrook, a friend of mine who is an English professor at Stanford and a published poet, to do an advanced version of the poetry portion of this exercise in executive programs at Stanford, where the students tend to be managers in technology-based companies. She introduces the participants to poetry in a minicourse consisting of readings, outside writing, and about four hours of lecture. Diane often begins by reading the group a poem, and even the process of listening to poetry being read causes them discomfort. Needless to say, their initial attempts at writing are painful. However, the beauty is there. Through a process of pleading, cajoling, explaining, praising, and criticizing, as well as the application of understanding and humor, Diane coaxes the reluctant group to write increasingly sophisticated verse. The poems on the next page are short examples written by some of the participants. A few amateur poets and a great change in everyone's viewpoint toward their own poetic abilities usually result from the experience of taking the minicourse.

Many people who feel terribly inadequate writing poetry are capable of constructing acceptable verse. They are merely suffering from lack of confidence in their own ability and the remnants of the social climate that inhibited poetry in high school. Similarly, awkwardness with drawing may result from a confusion between the type of drawing that most people do and the drawing of professional artists; awkwardness with math may result from that long-ago day when a relative lack of speed in calculation (which does not have that much to do with mathematics) caused one to slide from one's rightful spot at the head of the third grade class.

I am sometimes amused at the creativity and energy people will expend in order to avoid a particular style of problem solving with which they do not feel comfortable. A student submitted the short poem on love shown below. Clever, but probably more taxing than writing the poem.

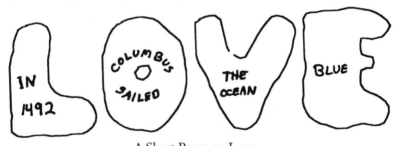

A Short Poem on Love

Another student submitted a paper in response to the desk lamp assignment. It began, "Before you can appreciate my desk-lamp design, it is essential that you understand a few concepts from circuit design, solid state theory, and optics" (obviously a high-tech desk lamp). This was followed by five pages of information from circuit design, solid state theory, and optical theory. However, there was no lamp design. After spending the alloted time telling me what he knew, the student conveniently avoided the process of visual imagery.

Shapely brown bicycling legs
Flashing in the sun through Stanford arches
I am an old man

I comb my hairs with a ball point pen
aging ego
hostage to ratted locks

Fern Hill, you stir the little boy
Take me back
Leave me by the stream above the cliffs
Let me relive the year
The joy; my friends; my dog
. . . no chores!

economic elements of engineering arouse
    me, Anne
eleemosynary music modifies my
    arousal, Anne
elegant eulogies/expert algorithims/
    integrated implantation
    Anne, Anne, Anne

Cherub face glowing to the world,
inner thoughts not expressed.
A filling sponge, thirsty.

Cold night falls on deeps now
narrow path lit by full moon
Dog barks into silence

Paint the sky
Roll the meadow
Fathom the depths
Water under the bridge
No U turn!

Personal perks, privileges.
Mission seduced integrity.
Beguiled by a lofty
Self-esteem through arrogance
Clouded vision. Exquisite
Rationalization. A
Talent squandered, a life disrupted.
Power corrupts.

Invent bad verse—why?
To manifest our joy
before this episode ends

Poems by Students in a Stanford Engineering Executive Program.

I clearly remember the response of an alumnus of Stanford to a math puzzle involving two trains. The puzzle hypothesized two trains one mile apart on a single straight track, each traveling at ten miles per hour toward the other. A fly, which had been riding on the front of one, takes off and flies toward the other at twenty miles per hour. Upon reaching the other (which is now less than one mile from the first train), the fly instantly turns and flies back to its original train, at which point it instantly turns again, etc., etc., etc. The puzzle asks how far the fly flies before it is crushed in the train collision. This puzzle obviously has to do with mathematics. Like the one in the exercise, however, it requires insight. The one in the exercise is best approached by imagining that the room is folded out flat as shown below. If you remember the Pythagorean theorem for a triangle, the answer can be seen to be forty feet. This requires memory. However, the problem with the fly and the train is straight-forward. It is merely necessary to realize that each train will travel one-half mile before they collide. Since the trains are traveling ten miles per hour, this will require 1/20th of an hour. The fly is traveling twenty miles per hour. In 1/20th of an hour the fly will fly one mile. However, the answer from the alumnus was:

> Free capricious soaring fly,
> why oh why
> did you have to die?

Once again, a rather wonderful answer to the problem. In fact, just the type of thing I would like to see people do in classes and workshops emphasiz-

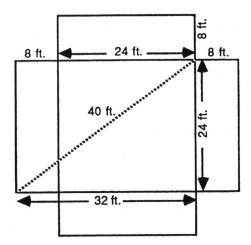

The Shortest Possible Path to the Crumb

ing creativity. However, I suspect that the motivation here was not so much creativity as a desire to not spend the time thinking mathematically.

Our habitual choice of problem-solving languages (use the one we are good at and enjoy, not necessarily the one that can best solve the problem) can be consciously overcome, with resulting increase in creative ability. The bad news is that overcoming habits is not easy. It requires first of all overcoming emotional signals and secondly, becom-ing more of a novice than we are used to being. The process is well known. Think of changing a tennis swing. You first come to realize that your swing is not all you might wish. Either your opponents are destroying you, or after studious viewing of television you find that Venus Williams has a more effective serve than yours, or someone you respect comments on the deplorable state of your backhand. Usually the first step in modifying habits is an indication that present habits are not adequate.

The next part of habit modification involves conscious and usually analytical activity. You take lessons, read books, watch videotapes and other tennis players, and learn as much as you can about the "form" you would like as well as the one you presently possess. You then consciously build your new habit. Although it may feel extraordinarily awkward at first, it will presumably take you where you want to go. Finally, you practice your new habit until it becomes a natural and programmed act in its own rights. This, of course, does not guarantee a lifetime of satisfaction and winning tennis games. It only means that you are set until the process begins again.

Naturally, such things as reward, punishment, and other types of motivational considerations are important in the process of habit modification. Also involved are time, energy, and perhaps money. However for the purpose of this discussion, the main thing to note is the centrality of the conscious in modifying habits. Not only is it effective, it is the *only* thing we have to modify habits.

David Straus and Michael Doyle are two people that have long been interested in problem-solving. At one time they founded a company entitled Interaction Associates that trained facilitators for problem-solving groups, offered educational programs, and conducted research in problem-solving. In one of their publications they explained:

> Each physical action or operation that we make to solve a problem can be seen in terms of a more general conceptual approach, useful in solving any problem. It is the rationale or purpose behind your actions: the

"why" as opposed to the "what." This general, conceptual approach we call a "strategy." In our terms, the concept inherent in a strategy is independent of context. In other words, a strategy should be able to be used in almost all kinds of problems. We find that the strategic level is one of the most useful ways of talking about problem-solving.

## Flexibility in Your Use of Strategies

One of their major techniques when working with groups was to keep track of the strategy or strategies being used at any time during a problem-solving session and to suggest changes or additions if the process appeared to be bogging down or overlooking possible approaches to solutions. In another of their publications they listed some 66 strategies, accompanying each with a description of the strategy, a list of its advantages and disadvantages and a sample exercise. A list of these strategies is shown below, along with a sample page taken from a document entitled "Strategy Notebook," which their company published.

| | | |
|---|---|---|
| Build up | Display | Simulate |
| Eliminate | Organize | Test |
| Work Forward | List | Play |
| Work Backward | Check | Manipulate |
| Associate | Diagram | Copy |
| Classify | Chart | Interpret |
| Generalize | Verbalize | Transform |
| Exemplify | Visualize | Translate |
| Compare | Memorize | Expand |
| Relate | Recall | Reduce |
| Commit | Record | Exaggerate |
| Defer | Retrieve | Understate |
| Leap In | Search | Adapt |
| Hold Back | Select | Substitute |
| Focus | Plan | Combine |
| Release | Predict | Separate |
| Force | Assume | Change |
| Relax | Question | Vary |
| Dream | Hypothesize | Cycle |
| Imagine | Guess | Repeat |
| Purge | Define | Systemize |
| Incubate | Symbolize | Randomize |

## Eliminate

POWERS   The power of elimination lies in the possibility that you may be more sure of what you don't want than what you do want. This strategy requires beginning with more than you need or want in the solution and eliminating elements according to some determined criteria. There is an element of safety in this strategy because you have not overly extended yourself by deciding what you don't want in the solution.

LIMITATIONS   This strategy assumes that within the realm of possibilities you are considering, there is a good solution. However, after you've finished eliminating, it's possible to end up with nothing. Another difficulty is that it is easy to infer that you want the opposite of what you have eliminated (i.e., you don't want rain, therefore you must want sunshine, leaving out the possibilities of snow, fog, hail, etc.). Thus elimination must be tempered by caution and good judgment.

EXERCISE—I GOT RELIGION   Have each member of your group build upon the subject of religion. Each member should offer any ideas or associations he has with the subject, and the ideas should be recorded. Once the group is satisfied that they have exhausted their resources, each member of the group should take a piece of paper and a pencil and review the recorded list, eliminating whatever they don't want included in their personal religion or philosophy, and writing down on their lists anything that is left. Once everyone has finished, pin the sheets of paper to a display board so that the members of the group can share each other's ideas. This exercise has the advantage of allowing the participants to get personally involved in the subject matter through use of the strategy of elimination. The exercise can also be modified to encompass a variety of subjects. This may prove to be an effective introductory experience for a humanities or comparative religion class.

Most people, as explained by Straus and Doyle, have no trouble in understanding such problem-solving strategies, once definitions and examples are made available. In fact, most people have *unconsciously* used all of them at one time or another. However, since the mind is used to selecting strategies subconsciously, it takes awareness of these strategies and *conscious* choice or an outside facilitator to make the best use of them on a specific problem. The Introduction to *Process Notebook*, also by Interaction Associates, summarized the situation as follows:

> Just as we use physical tools for physical tasks, we employ conceptual tools for conceptual tasks. To familiarize yourself with a tool, you may experiment with it, test it in different situations, and evaluate its usefulness. The same method can be applied to conceptual tools. Our ability as thinkers is dependent on our range and skill with our own tools.

It is obvious that a compromise has to be reached in the conscious selection of thinking modes and problem-solving strategies. You should not devote 95 percent of your mental energy to the selection of strategies and thinking modes and reserve only 5 percent for the solving of the problem. Yet you should certainly spend some conscious effort thinking about strategies. First, by selecting strategies consciously you can often find approaches you would never have known about had you left the selection to your subconscious. Second, by becoming aware of various thinking strategies, what they can do, and how to use them, you can ensure that the mind has a larger selection when it utilizes its subconscious selection method. You can essentially become your own "facilitator."

## The Computer

Interesting cases of intellectual inflexibility can be seen in the use of the computer. Society has accepted the computer, but many individuals are still suspicious of it and reluctant to use it. It is a very powerful thinking tool. Not to take full advantage of it is a disadvantage. Other people, the cyber people we referred to in the last chapter, seem to almost worship it and become completely chained to the intricacies of the Internet and new software and hardware products. Unless you work as a computer system consultant, this is also a disadvantage. If you like gadgets and games, you can spend all of your time simply messing with computers rather than utilizing them to solve problems. This may be fun, but one could hardly call it a meaningful contribution to the human condition.

Clifford Stoll, who has worked with computers since he built his first Altair kit in the 1970's, wrote an amusing book a few years ago entitled *Silicon Snake Oil*. It is a critique of computers and at one point in the book he complains about the large portion of his time that he spends trying to get his computer to do what he wants it to do. In his mind, this situation is not improving and by now we shouldn't have to spend so much time fighting our systems. I agree with him, as do most computer users I know. When your computer crashes or gives you some strange error message it not only takes time to coax it back to happiness, but also breaks your train of thought.

Computers affected my professional life early, since when I worked there, the Jet Propulsion Laboratory was using large (in those days) computer-based structural analysis programs, and relatively primitive computers were included in spacecraft to do onboard guidance, control, and scientific data reduction. I dutifully bought a TRS 80, one of the first IBM PCs and an Apple I and tried to apply them to my life. I now rely upon a great deal of digital computer and communication equipment which allow me to be much more effective than I used to be, but I am not a computer expert and do not want to become one. To me the problem is one of balance. How do you make the best use of the "digital revolution"? Computers can be a great aid to creativity, but perhaps the greatest inhibition to personal creativity is lack of time, and if computers soak up too much time, they can inhibit creativity.

## Importance of Correct Information

Lack of, or incorrect, information is a third intellectual block. As we discussed earlier, Arthur Koestler in "The Three Domains of Creativity" states: "The creative act consists in combining previously unrelated structures in such a way that you get more out of the emergent whole than you have put in." Other definitions of creativity also emphasize this "combining" aspect. Plainly we must have the components to combine (information). But let us look at what happens if some of our components are incorrect. We will consider a situation in which each component appears no more than once and in which the order of combination is important.

If we combine two quantities, *a* and *b*, we have four possible results (*a*, *b*, *ab*, and *ba*). If *a* is incorrect, three of these results contain erroneous information. If both *a* and *b* are incorrect, all of them are contaminated. If we combine three quantities, *a*, *b*, and *c*, we have 15 possible results (*abc, acb, bac, bca, cab, cba, ab, ba, ac, ca, bc, cb, a, b, c*). If *a* is incorrect, 11 of these results contain erroneous information. If both *a* and *b* are incorrect, 14 of them are wrong. By playing with a little mathematics, we can come up with a general expression for this contamination tendency and create the following table that indicates the advantages of correct information to the problem solver.

The first column represents the number of elements available to combine as Mr. Koestler would like us to. The second column indicates the number of arrangements available from this number of elements. The third column gives the number of arrangements which contain erroneous information if one of the elements (*a*) contains error. The fourth column gives this number if two of the elements (*a* and *b*) contain error.

| n | Possible arrangements | Erroneous if *a* is wrong | Erroneous if *a* and *b* are wrong |
|---|---|---|---|
| 1 | 1 | 1 | |
| 2 | 4 | 3 | 4 |
| 3 | 15 | 11 | 14 |
| 4 | 64 | 49 | 60 |
| 5 | 325 | 261 | 310 |
| 6 | 1,956 | 1,631 | 1,892 |
| 7 | 13,699 | 11,743 | 13,374 |
| 8 | 109,600 | 95,901 | 107,644 |
| 9 | 986,409 | 876,809 | 972,710 |
| 10 | 9,864,100 | 8,877,691 | 9,754,500 |

These simple-minded numbers are not intended to be a model of conceptualization. I merely throw them in to demonstrate how rapidly combinations containing erroneous information build up as incorrect elements are introduced.

During the solution of a problem correct and adequate information is, of course, extremely important. An intellectual block that may prevent the problem-solver from acquiring well-balanced and pertinent information can be disastrous. Mechanical engineers with a block against electrical engineering or electrical engineers with a block against mechanical engineering may design strange things, such as mechanical television sets or complex electrical power transmission systems where simple mechanical ones would be cheaper and more reliable. People who consistently resist utilizing mathematics limit their problem-solving abilities by being blocked from useful quantitative data. Just as people who are blocked against considering aesthetic, emotional, and qualitative inputs in their decision-making also limit their problem-solving capabilities by refusing to acquire often useful information. Engineers who are uncomfortable with aesthetics can make outstandingly inhumane and ugly devices which may, as a side issue, not even sell well. Environmentalists who ignore the use of quantitative facts and statistics cannot be very productive in designing effective solutions to environmental problems.

There is, however, disagreement as to whether information is universally valuable at all phases of problem-solving. One school of thought maintains that one of the worst enemies of innovation is the large impact of existing solutions on conceptual thinking. This is the school that says: "It is difficult to think of alternate methods of felling small trees if you have spent a lot of time swinging an axe." I know one extremely inventive engineer who finds it very important to operate with a "clean" mind—he avoids learning anything about previous, related solutions to his problems. However, I know another equally productive engineer who spends a great deal of effort learning everything she can about every previous development that seems even slightly related to her problem (a "dirty" mind?). It is true that if you do not know about axes, your solution to felling small trees may be reinventing the axe. You are also denied the use of the axe as a source of additional concepts.

In my opinion, the optimal situation in problem-solving is to be able to use a clean-minded approach to a problem, even though your mind is stuffed with information. I am, of course, biased by my own preferences. As I previously admitted, I grunt my way through problems instead of solving them in an effortless flash of insight. The more information I have about the problem and previous attempts to solve it, the better I do. However, it is sometimes necessary in the problem-solving process to hold this information at arm's length. Certainly, for instance, a massive amount of information is necessary when working with high technology, complex business situations, or interpersonal interactions. However, this abundant information can often prevent you from seeing very elegant solutions. Information makes you an expert, and William J. J. Gordon in *Synectics* says this about expertise: "The specialized semantics of established knowledge constitutes conventions which make reality abstract and secondhand. Learned conventions can be windowless fortresses which exclude viewing the world in new ways."

I believe that it is possible to be an expert and still view the world in new ways. One does not need someone who grew up alone on a desert island to invent a better can opener. One can use people who not only are quite knowledgeable about electrical, mechanical, physical, chemical, and whatever other phenomena, but who also have been closely associated with presently existing can openers. It is only necessary that these people be able to view the world in new ways in spite of all of their prior knowledge. If they can do this, they should do better than someone from a desert island.

## Expressive Blocks

Turning now to expressive blocks, let us begin by doing another simple exercise.

> **Exercise:** This will require you to find (or make) a simple object whose shape cannot be described by a common name. It could be a block with a corner cut off and a groove along one face, a part from a machine, or any other object with a simple yet irregular three-dimensional shape. Do not use a pencil, a pair of scissors, a tonic water bottle, or other object which is so utilitarian and well known that its shape is familiar to everyone. Find several people, place the object you have chosen in a large paper bag, and have one of the people place his hand in the bag, without looking at the object. He is to describe the object to the other people, who are to draw it.

This exercise is surprisingly difficult. The lack of feedback in the communication loop is of course a contributor to this. Some feedback can be obtained by allowing those drawing the object to ask questions of the describer, although the exercise is most impressive when questions are not allowed. The exercise is also difficult because it is not easy to identify shapes by feel. However, the chief difficulty is probably that of describing a physical object verbally. If your volunteers are mathematically oriented and communicate in terms of x-y-z-coordinates or other geometrical surface description techniques, they will do better at this task. However, if the common verbal approach is used (e.g., "the bottom is a rectangular place with the corner cut off, and then there is a short side going up from the cut-off corner") the task is abysmally difficult. Another reason for the difficulty of the exercise is the rather low level of drawing talent developed in most people. Even if the shape could be perfectly described verbally, most people do not have the faculty capture it on paper.

I usually do this exercise with a large group so that I can compare drawings after it is over (try it at a party). The presence of the audience adds some interesting emotional blocks. The person describing the object will do better if he or she spends some time feeling the object before describing it. However, it is difficult to spend this time in front of an impatient crowd. The person usually will plunge right into describing. The description will usually proceed at a rapid rate (even though the audience may be picking up no information of use) as the describer usually feels somewhat embarrassed standing in front of a group with his hand in a bag doing what to him may seem a trivial task.

Since he will think he has a good idea of the shape of the object (he has his hand on it), he will find it difficult to believe that the audience does not. He may become impatient. He will undoubtedly demonstrate a form of incubation by thinking of a better way to have done his task after the exercise is over.

This exercise demonstrates both the use of *inadequate language skill* to express an idea and the *imprecision in our verbal expression*. It is an extremely common block that one finds often, for instance, in the engineering profession. Many students and engineers are not fond of drawing, partly because they may find it difficult and partly because in some fields drafting has somehow been given a lower status than, say, analysis. We find continual attempts, therefore, to communicate geometrical ideas verbally. Often the degree of difficulty induced by this expressive block is not even appreciated, since the describer knows exactly what he is trying to describe, and the describee often naturally assumes that she understands exactly what the other person is describing. Another problem that demonstrates this block of imprecise verbal expression (if you have access to a dozen people or so) is the following:

> **Exercise:** Give a person a drawing of a simple object (once again an abstract object so a name does not describe its shape). Ask them to look at it awhile and then describe it verbally to another person. The second person should then describe it verbally to a third person, and so on. This should be done in a manner so that the others in the group cannot overhear the descriptions. When the description of the object has been passed through ten people or so, have one last person draw the object. Comparison of the final drawing with the original drawing should prove fascinating.

I often use this game in classes. The following figure shows a simple object (it is an engineering drawing, but the people playing the game were students in an engineering class). The figure on the next page shows some of the results. There was obviously some error.

One of the difficult things in both of these exercises is that communication is one-way. This type of communication is amazingly weak unless the receiver has the same information in mind as the sender, which is unlikely in situations involving creativity. If two-way communication is allowed in the exercises (receivers can ask questions) the process is much more accurate, but agonizingly slow.

Are there other reasons why communication may be difficult in situations involving creativity? Sure, they are easy to find—the frustration

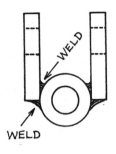
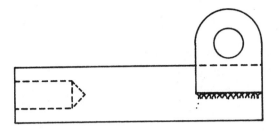

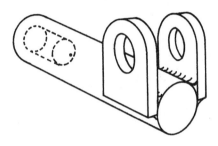

of trying to present concepts in a foreign language, the frustration of the writer when his computer is broken, the frustration of the executive whose administrative assistant is sick, the frustration of the technically trained person trying to explain quantitative concepts to one who hates mathematics.

In situations involving creativity we often benefit by combining disciplines in new ways. Communication across disciplines is unusually difficult because our mind is not particularly eager to learn new jargon and techniques, or to admit that we need to do so. We are afraid that our need to learn new information will be interpreted (mistakenly) as a sign of ignorance. One of the great challenges in teaching is that one cannot rely upon students to ask questions when they do not understand things. It is quite easy to lose an entire class (usually if one student does not understand, the others don't either) with no indication. One of the common explanations for this reluctance to ask questions is that asking questions is admitting ignorance.

I used to be called a systems engineer. When I was in the US Air Force, the military had just discovered the "systems" concept. No

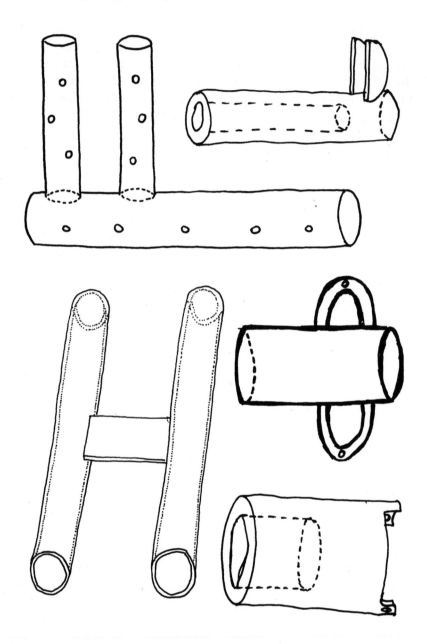

longer would there be an airplane, ammunition, starting carts, and a plug for the Pitot tube. Now there would be a weapon system. People began to talk in terms of the systems concept, systems management, systems approach, and, of course, systems engineering. Companies such as Ramo-Woolridge (the RW of TRW) leapt to prominence because of their systems design and management ability. This approach instantly infiltrated the aerospace industry, so that by the time I joined the Jet Propulsion Laboratory in 1959 it was known that a systems approach was necessary to design something as complex as a spacecraft. There was some dissension from certain senior people who considered systems engineering to be just plain old good engineering, but we youngsters leapt on it with enthusiasm. I was a systems engineer for a while at JPL and later taught systems engineering at Stanford and spent a large portion of my summers for ten years in a NASA-sponsored program, which attempted to give engineering professors a better feel for systems engineering.

What is systems engineering? Just plain old good engineering. However, it has evolved its own philosophies and exists as a field because of the difficulty of communicating across different jargons, perceptions of importance, and perspectives in different technical fields. The communication engineers see nothing wrong with leaving an extra 3 db margin in their system, even though some poor mechanical engineer may end up trying to design an antenna with twice the area as a result.

Interdisciplinary communication is not restricted to technological companies. Any organization has difficulties with communication between the various specialized groups within it, and any family has difficulty with communication between members exercising different roles in the family. The traditional housewife (should any still exist) has as much difficulty communicating with the traditional husband (none still exist), because of the difference in their experiences, perceived priorities, and responsibilities.

The message here is a simple but important one. In situations involving change and creativity, communication cannot be taken for granted. Efforts must be made to ensure that communications are two way and that adequate time and effort are taken to convey the information. It is also worthwhile to be suspicious as to difficulties due to changes in the disciplinary mix. Finally, priorities and values will perhaps need changing, and intensive communication is sometimes necessary to achieve this. In particular, a great amount of communication is required to convince people who have played a particular role for a long period of time to change their role. In such cases, expressive blocks can be crippling.

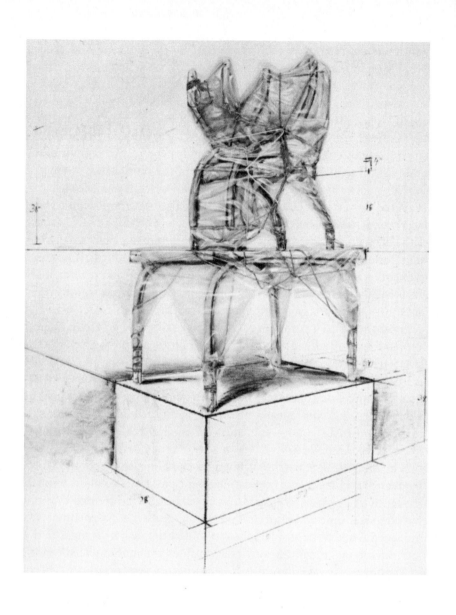

## CHAPTER SIX

# Alternate Thinking Languages

IN CHAPTER FIVE WE DISCUSSED the conceptual block from the improper choice of a problem-solving "language." In this chapter, I would like to elaborate on this point. The well-armed problem-finder/solver is fluent in many mental languages and is able to use them interchangeably to record information, communicate with the unconscious, and consciously manipulate. Some of these moves are more "natural" to us than others. They are often even more powerful when used in combination with each other than when used alone.

In this chapter I will discuss some of these thinking modes or languages and put in a plug for some that I do not think receive their fair share of emphasis. To introduce this discussion, let me give you the following exercise:

> **Exercise:** Imagine that you just gave a ride to a hitchhiker who turned out to be an eccentric wealthy builder. As a token of his gratitude, he offers to build an addition onto your house according to your specifications, asking only that the total budget not exceed $40,000. Conceptualize the addition you would ask him to build for you. As you work on this problem try to observe what is going on in your mind (concerning the addition, not the probability of the situation occuring).

Once again, you should have become aware of the difficulty in observing your thinking process as it swings back and forth between the conscious and the unconscious. However, were you roughly aware of what "languages" you employed? Did you think verbally? Quantitatively? Pictorially? Did you imagine smells? Sounds? Tactile sensations? Muscle sensations? Did you tend to work mostly in one language?

If you are typical of most people, you will most easily recall the thinking you did that was in a verbal mode. Verbal thinking is the most prestigious (and perhaps most common) mental language in our culture.

Many psychologists and general semanticists feel that verbal languages are the basis of thinking. For instance, L. S. Vygotsky, in *Thought and Language*, says, "Thought is born through words." Edward Sapir in *Language* says that "language and our thought grooves are inextricably interwoven, are, in a sense, one and the same." Our educational systems reinforce this bias. As Rudolf Arnheim says in his essay "Visual Thinking," in *Education of Vision* (edited by G. Kepes): "In our schools, reading, writing, and arithmetic are practiced as skills that detach the child from sensory (as opposed to verbal or mathematical) experience. . . . Only in kindergarten and first grade is education based on the cooperation of all the essential powers of the mind. Thereafter this natural and sensible procedure is dismissed as an obstacle to training in the proper kind of abstraction." In our culture, we find much emphasis on reading speed and comprehension, on I.Q. tests which rely heavily on verbal ability, and on the use of verbal aptitude scores as an extremely important indicator of intelligence relating to academic and professional potential.

Being a verbal person, I would be one of the last to impugn the sagacity of those who would sanctify the word. It is certainly true that many problems can be well solved verbally. Such solutions can then be easily communicated through well-established verbal channels. However, as we saw in our monk puzzle and our paper-folding problem, there are also problems that can be solved verbally only with great difficulty. With this in mind consider the following problems.

> **Problem One:** Bob has three times as many pine cones as Dan. Between them they have 28 pine cones. How many does each have?

This problem can be worked verbally with the aid of logic, using a trial and error approach between the alternative possibilities. The solution to the problem is relatively simple. It can be solved algebraically as follows:

> let $b$ stand for the number of Bob's pine cones
> let $d$ stand for the number of Dan's pine cones

We know that the following relationships hold:

$$(1)\ b + d = 28$$
$$(2)\ b = 3d$$

Plugging in the second into the first and collecting terms, we find that $4d = 28$. Dan must therefore have 7 pine cones and Bob 21.

For any of you familiar with algebra, the mathematics involved here is trivial. Most of you, algebraic or not, are probably able to solve problems like this without too much distress. However, consider the next problem.

> **Problem Two:** Mary has three times as many pine cones as the pine cones owned by both Nora and Oscar. Dan has two times as many pine cones as Bob. Mary has one-and-a-half times as many pine cones as Dan. Oscar and Dan together have as many pine cones as the number Nora has plus twice the number Bob has. Bob, Dan, Mary, Nora, and Oscar have 28 pine cones between them. How many does each have?

I warn that if you are not familiar with algebra, this one will cause you a bit more distress. With sufficient trial and error work, it can be solved through logical verbal thought. However, the amount of work and bookkeeping is annoying, considering the unprofound nature of the problem. A mathematical approach is clearly advantageous. It can be solved algebraically as follows.

As we did before, let the number of Mary's pine cones be "$m$," the number of Nora's be "$n$," and the number of Oscar's "$o$." The relationships between these numbers (including Dan's "$d$" and Bob's "$b$") are:

$$(1)\ m = 3(n + o)$$
$$(2)\ d = 2b$$
$$(3)\ m = 3/2\ d$$
$$(4)\ o + d = n + 2b$$
$$(5)\ b + d + m + n + o = 28$$

As the mathematicians among you realize, these relationships give us enough equations to allow us to solve for all of the unknown numbers. A way (not the only way) to solve these is to first of all substitute the value for $n + o$ shown in relationship (1) into relationship (5), [i.e., $n + o = m/3$]. This gives:

$$b + d + 4/3\ m = 28$$

From relationship (2), we can see that $b = d/2$. Substituting this into the above, we get:

$$3/2\ d + 4/3\ m = 28$$

Relationship (3), however, tells us that $m = 3/2\ d$. Substituting this into our expression, we now get:

$$7/2\ d = 28$$
$$d = 8$$

Hence, Dan has 8 pine cones. Knowing this, we can then happily return to our original relationships and find that Bob has 4 pine cones [from relationship (2)], Mary has 12 [from (3)], and Nora and Oscar together have 4 [from relationship (5)]. Since relationship (4) now tells us that Oscar and Nora have the same number of pine cones, they have 2 each.

Some very simple mathematical language therefore leads us to an answer that requires a good bit of pain to reach verbally. Now you're ready for our third problem.

> **Problem Three:** Suppose that Nora, in a fit of pique, finds a ladder with which she plans to acquire as many pine cones as Mary. The ladder is 10 feet long and the tree trunk is vertical. Just as Nora reaches the top step of the ladder, it begins slipping. Suppose we wanted to know how fast Nora is dropping when the base of the ladder is 6 feet from the tree and is skidding along the ground at 5 feet per second, as shown below.

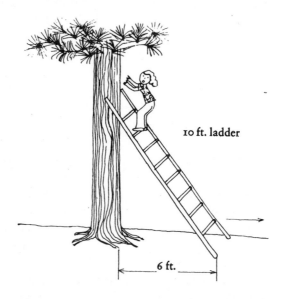

10 ft. ladder

6 ft.

How would you do on this one verbally? Probably not well at all because there is very little to guide you, and a trial and error approach is difficult. Once again, mathematically it is simple, requiring only a trace of trigonometry and calculus. If you abstract the situation as follows:

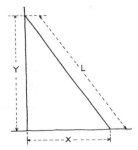

and call the distance from the base of the tree to the base of the ladder $x$ and the distance from the ground to the top of the ladder $y$, you can apply the theorem of Mr. Pythagoras to write the relationships between these two quantities and the ladder length as:

$$x^2 + y^2 = l^2$$

Substituting 6 feet for $x$ and 10 feet for $l$, we find that $y$ is 8 feet. Now if we differentiate (a basic calculus operation) this relationship with respect to time, we get:

$$2x\dot{x} + 2y\dot{y} = 0$$

where the dotted quantities are velocities. Substituting 6 feet for $x$, 8 feet for $y$, and 5 feet per second for $\dot{x}$, we find that $\dot{y}$ (the quantity we want) is 3¾ feet per second. Once again, simple in the mathematical language—difficult in the verbal.

Clearly, if you attempt to predict the behavior of objects in space, components of complicated machines or structures, or populations and resources, you must include mathematics among your thinking modes. If you cook from recipes, balance your bank account, or use the directions on your lawn fertilizer, you must also use mathematics. If you do not use mathematics as a thinking mode, you are handicapped in working with problems that demand quantification.

Although mathematical aptitude and performance are highly respected in certain circles in our society, verbal aptitude and performance are more generally admired. In fact, in some circles, mathematical illiteracy seems to be a desirable characteristic. Some people seem to feel the cultural need to reject mathematics and boast about their ineptness with quantitative matters. Some eschew mathematics as though it were automatic and without soul, a misconception, of course, since pure mathematicians are motivated and guided by a highly developed sense of aesthetics. Still, mathematicians are heavily stereotyped in the U.S., and mathematical fluency is much less important than verbal glibness in the majority of high-reward positions in this country. For instance, were I to run for the office of President of the U.S. (assuming that this is a high-reward position), I would probably not challenge my opponent to a mathematical problem-solving contest on national TV. In fact, if anything, I would probably conceal my mathematical ability in order not to lose the votes of all those who rejected math as disagreeable in their childhood.

If more people would utilize mathematics in problem-solving (even at a low level of competence), the overall quality of solutions would benefit. Mathematical and verbal thinking together allow much more powerful attacks on problems than verbal thinking alone. I will not further elaborate on the usefulness of mathematical thinking, since it is generally accepted. I discussed verbal and mathematical thinking rather to demonstrate that two thinking "languages" make one a more potent and sophisticated problem-solver, and that some languages are in higher repute (and more frequently relied upon) than others.

Discomfort with mathematics also probably results in discomfort with technology and the natural and social sciences, since they are heavy users of mathematics. The "scientific illiteracy" and "technological illiteracy" that the media is so fond of writing about can result. This is sometimes blamed for everything from economic ills to loss of intellectual pleasure. It can certainly result in a loss of creativity. Science and technology are integral to our way of thinking, our industrial success, our health, and the quality of our lives. To avoid them professionally is difficult and may hamper one's effectiveness. To avoid them because of negative emotional reactions is a loss and a reason for a bit of self-analysis and perhaps study.

Let me now discuss some other languages that are extremely valuable in conceptualization. These are the languages of the senses: sight, sound, taste, smell and touch.

## Visual Thinking

A particularly important mode of thinking, which I have referred to several times before and which is presently receiving increased attention academically, is visual thinking. Visualization is an important thinking mode which is especially useful in solving problems where shapes, forms, or patterns are concerned. In his book *Visual Thinking* Rudolf Arnheim explains: "Visual thinking is constantly used by everybody. It directs figures on a chess board and designs global politics on the geographical map. Two dexterous moving men steering a piano along a winding staircase think visually in an intricate sequence of lifting, shifting, and turning . . . ." All of us are used to using visual imagery in some situations. For instance, visual imagery is extremely common in dreams. It is also common if someone asks us a question about the appearance of a person or a place. But it is also used in conceptualization, at times when you would not obviously expect its use.

In *The Act of Creation* Koestler quotes Friedrich Kekule, the famous chemist who discovered the structure of the benzene ring in a dream after having devoted a great deal of conscious thought to its enigmatic structure. Kekule describes the discovery:

> I turned my chair to the fire and dozed. Again the atoms were gamboling before my eyes. This time the smaller groups kept modestly in the background. My mental eye, rendered more acute by repeated visions of this kind, could now distinguish larger structures, of manifold conformation; long rows, sometimes more closely fitted together; all twining and twisting in snakelike motion. But look! What was that? One of the snakes had seized hold of its own tail, and the form whirled mockingly before my eyes. As if by a flash of lightning, I awoke.

The result of the dream was Kekule's brilliant insight that organic compounds such as benzene were *closed rings* rather than open structures.

In *Experiences in Visual Thinking* Bob McKim writes of three kinds of visual imagery that are necessary in effective visual thinking. The first, *perceptual imagery*, is sensory experience of the physical world; it is what one sees and records in his brain. The second is *mental imagery*, which is constructed in the mind and utilizes information recorded from perceptual imagery. The third type is *graphic imagery*. This is imagery that is sketched, doodled, drawn, or otherwise put down in a written communicable form, either to aid in your own process of thinking or to aid in communication with others.

Let us first of all briefly consider perceptual imagery, or seeing. By asking you to draw a telephone keyboard in Chapter Two, I hope I convinced you that you do not record everything you look at, at least at an accessible level (under hypnosis, you might be enabled to draw the buttons on a telephone properly). People see poorly for several reasons. As previously mentioned, one reason is an oversaturation of input. Another is lack of motivation. People tend to see better those things which are more important to them, more unusual, or of an easily-recorded visual character.

You can learn to see better through conscious effort, especially if you are convinced that seeing better is important to you. One way of rapidly developing your *seeing* ability is to engage in activities where you must reproduce things you have seen.

> **Exercise:** You can exercise your seeing ability by looking at things and then drawing them. Such an activity requires not only seeing but imagining and drawing, which will be discussed later. Try this procedure with objects around you, or better yet, objects in your profession that you think it would be helpful to know more about.

A drawing course can improve your seeing ability. If you have to draw trees, you will really start seeing them. I took an art course once in which the teacher took delight in asking us to make quick sketches of friends, family, pets, home, and neighborhood. I found this extremely interesting because I looked at my immediate environment at least two orders of magnitude more closely. One of my colleagues took a photography course in which the instructor taught the students to photograph scenery by taking a jar of beans and the students into a field, throwing a bean into the field for each member of the class, and then telling each student to stand on his bean and spend the day shooting scenic pictures. Such exercises *make* you see. You can take pictures of the Grand Canyon or other scenic wonders without putting a great deal of effort into detailed seeing. However, taking a beautiful picture while standing on your bean in a field requires that you truly use your powers of visual perception.

Now let us talk about the second type of visualization: mental imagery. These mental images are probably the most important for the conceptualizer. According to McKim, there are two aspects of visual imagery which are important. The first he calls clarity (how sharp and filled with detail are the images?). The second he calls control (how well can you manipulate them?). Here is an exercise to let you evaluate your visual "imaging" capability.

> **Exercise:** *Clarity of Mental Images.* Imagine the following. After each mark a clear (c), vague (v), or nothing (n) in accordance with how clear (sharp and detailed) the image appears in your mind.

1. The face of a friend
2. Your kitchen
3. The grille on the front of your car
4. A camellia blossom
5. A fiddler crab
6. A Boeing 747
7. A running cow
8. The earth from orbit
9. Your first car
10. Bill Clinton

The clarity of your mental images depends upon several factors. First of all, in this type of exercise, it depends on *seeing*. If you have never seen a fiddler crab or a running cow, your mental images were probably not too sharp. It also depends on your seeing *ability*. And this in turn, as we have mentioned, depends on motivation (your camellia was probably clearer if you are a camellia freak), the visual character of the object (Bill Clinton was probably fairly clear because he has been characterized so often in the news and in political cartoons), timing (your first car may have grown dim by now), and saturation (your car grille?). Finally, it depends upon the image-reproduction mechanism of your brain. There is certainly individual variation in the ability to visually imagine which goes beyond the variability mentioned above. If you ask a roomful of people to visualize a brick or an apple, and then ask individual members of the room questions about their image, you will get a range of answers, the clarity of which extends from images vivid in color, detail, texture, background, and shadows, to no particular image at all.

> **Exercise:** For your own information try visualizing a series of objects and see if you can determine a pattern in your own imaging ability. Are you better at visualizing people than objects? Or worse? Are you better at two-dimensional objects than three-dimensional? Are you better at small things than large things? Where do you see your image? Is it out in front of your eyes or back in your skull somewhere?

Visual imaging ability is complex, since it depends not only upon your ability to form images, but also upon the supply of pertinent imagery which is stored in the mind. However, it seems safe to say that you can improve your visual imaging capability by devoting effort to it and making it a higher priority item in problem-solving. Visual images can be consciously enhanced. When I was a student of John Arnold at

Stanford, he was constantly hitting me with "visualize an apple" type problems. As a result, I became so conditioned that when asked to visualize something, I still concentrate all of the information and energy I can on the task. Now let us look at your ability to *control* (manipulate) visual imagery.

> **Exercise:** Imagine the following:
>
> 1. A pot of water coming to a boil and boiling over
> 2. Your Boeing 747 being towed from the terminal, taxiing to the runway, waiting for a couple of other planes, and then taking off
> 3. Your running cow changing slowly into a galloping race-horse
> 4. An old person you know well changing back into a teenager
> 5. A speeding car colliding with a giant feather pillow
> 6. The image in (5)—in reverse

Are you better at manipulating images you have actually seen or in creating new ones? Can you modify images in a fantastic (non-real) way? Take some time, and see whether you can extend your understanding of your ability to control your visual imagery. Try manipulating various types of images, inventing images in your mind, etc. Many people feel that the ability to control visual images can be developed through practice. Bob McKim in *Experiences in Visual Thinking* discusses what he calls "directed fantasy" as a way of strengthening imagination. In "directed fantasy" the participant is asked to fantasize in a number of directions that take him through a wider range of imaginative activities. He is forced to "exercise" his imaginative abilities and confront imaginative blocks that he would ordinarily avoid. By finding that he is able to wander freely through these areas and allow his imagination to range widely without catastrophic results, he becomes encouraged to feel more familiar with the use of visual imagery in conceptualization.

Now let us discuss the third type of visualization—graphic imagery. In order to take full advantage of visual thinking ability, *drawing* is necessary. Drawing allows the recording, storage, manipulation, and communication of images to augment the pictures you can generate in your imagination. In the Design Division, we find it useful to divide drawing into two categories: that which is done to communicate with others, and that which is done to communicate with oneself. The following drawing is a type used generally for the purpose of communicating with others. It was drawn by architect Walter Thomason of San Francisco.

Drawings such as the following idea sketches are generally used in communicating with oneself. These were drawn by one of the founders

of Concept II, Peter Dreissigacker, when he was a Stanford engineering graduate student. (Yours need not be as artistic.)

The first type of drawing (communicative) receives a good bit of attention educationally, and you can learn to make such drawings through formal courses of instruction. The second type (thinking sketches) receives far less emphasis, yet it is an important adjunct to visual thinking. Given a large pad of paper and a pencil, most people will make sketches as they work on sample problem exercises. Strangely enough, the same people often will not go to the trouble of summoning their drawing materials on their own in a problem-solving situation.

I am probably sensitized to these particular problems because I have spent quite a bit of time teaching design in a university setting which attracts an extremely verbal group of students. A great deal of effort has been put into their verbal (and mathematical) abilities during their formal education, but little into their visual ability. When they come to Stanford, many are "visual illiterates." They often are not used to drawing, nor to using visual imagery as a thinking mode. Although their drawing is generally not good, it is usually good enough (especially with a few helpful hints) to use as a thinking aid. Nonetheless, they are usually extremely reluctant to draw because their drawings compare so badly with drawings made by professionals (intended for communication with others). In design, we try to encourage crude but informative drawings for the student's own purposes. We also try to encourage improving one's drawing skills, since we find that good drawing skill is a powerful conceptual aid. Try the following exercise and see whether your drawing skills (no matter how marginal) help you in conceptualizing:

> **Exercise:** Buy a cheap notebook of a convenient size (small enough to accompany you, but as big as possible otherwise) and provide yourself with the most satisfying line-maker you can find. (A good one is a Pentel-type pen, which looks like a ballpoint pen but has a tapered fiber tip that makes an instant dark and smooth line.) Make drawings for yourself in this notebook for the next week or so while you are conceptualizing and otherwise involved in solving problems. Your drawings may be doodles, block diagrams, schematics, squiggles, sketches, or what have you. Try to see which of these drawings (if any) help in problem-solving and which do not. Are they of more use in particular portions (e.g., at the beginning) of the problem-solving process? Does a lack of drawing-skill minimize their effect? Do you use your notebook to refer

to your previous work? Does the size of your notebook inhibit you? (If so change to newsprint or butcher paper on the wall or a table and to larger felt pens or to color, and try again.)

By emphasizing drawing as a thinking technique, I do not mean to belittle its power as a communication device. I have had many experiences in which people who are able to draw well have been able to influence others in a problem-solving situation, for better or worse. This is especially prevalent in design situations where no precedent exists. I was recently supervising a student group engaged in the design of a new type of underwater vehicle. One of the students was excellent at making quick renderings. Each time he would put forth a concept it would seem so real in its rendered form that the group would gleefully adopt it. Then, when he produced another concept the next day, the group would be in temporary consternation until they adopted the new one. I have seen the same thing happen many times in the design of spacecraft, where little visual precedent exists. A well-drawn concept has amazing power. Drawings, of course, also have amazing ability to convey precise information, even if crudely done. One of my oldest and best friends, for instance, is a farmer. When I visit him I often accompany him on his rounds. Since I am a helpful sort, I try to aid him in his various projects, which often consist of moving large inert objects. Such tasks should be straightforward to someone like me, who is, after all, an engineering professor. However, he gives directions verbally, with the result that I am always bewildered by a version of the situation we encountered in the block-in-the-bag exercise in Chapter Three. (I am on a long-term project of getting him to draw crude pictures for his people and for me, so I will not stupidly put things in the wrong place.)

> **Exercise:** Use your drawing skills, no matter how marginal, to aid you in giving directions to people. Carry a small pad and pencil to do this if necessary. You are probably familiar with drawing crude maps to show people how to get to your house. But have you ever drawn your children a map of where to pile the leaves they are raking up, your husband a map of how to put things away in the house, or your wife a map of how to carve a roast (sorry for any role typing)?

Let us now leave visual imagery, an extremely important tool in conceptualization. If you have the time and inclination to attempt to develop your visual thinking ability, the Web will give you places to start. At least become aware of your abilities and limitations with visual imagery and attempt to use visualization in your thinking process whenever appropriate. It is one of the most basic of all thinking modes and one that is *invaluable* in problem-solving.

## Other Sensory Languages

We will now go on to other sensory languages that are essential in conceptualization and are used even less frequently in general problem-solving than visual thinking. Just as visual imagery corresponds to the sense of sight, other types of sensory imagery also result from their corresponding senses.

Here are some exercises for you to test how good you are at different types of sensory imagery. Once again, rate them clear (c), vague (v), or nothing (n).

**Exercise:** Imagine:
The laugh of a friend
The sound of thunder
The sound of a horse walking on a road
The sound of a racing car
The feel of wet grass
The feel of your wife's/husband's/girlfriend's/boyfriend's/pet's hair
The feel of diving into a cold swimming pool
The feel of a runny nose
The smell of bread toasting
The smell of fish
The smell of gasoline
The smell of leaves burning
The taste of a pineapple
The taste of Tabasco sauce
The taste of toothpaste
The muscular sensation of pulling on a rope
The muscular sensation of throwing a rock
The muscular sensation of running
The muscular sensation of squatting
The sensation of being uncomfortably cold
The sensation of having eaten too much
The sensation of extreme happiness
The sensation of a long attack of hiccups

Now try the following for control of separate sensory images:

The sensation of being uncomfortably cold changing to one of being uncomfortably hot

The laugh of a friend changing into the sound of thunder

The feel of wet grass changing into the feel of your wife's/ husband's/girlfriend's/boyfriend's/pet's hair

The smell of fish changing into the smell of gasoline

The muscular sensation of pulling on a rope changing into the muscular sensation of rowing a boat

Such exercises have a function equivalent to the earlier exercises on visual imagery. They may help you develop your sensory imagery ability, if used extensively. In any case, they at least let you learn more about your ability to image in various sensory languages.

Sight tends to be the predominant sense from a physiological standpoint. However, just as verbal thinking should not be allowed to elbow visual thinking out of the way, neither should the visual mode be allowed to overpower other sensory modes. Smell, sound, taste, and touch are extremely important to problem-solvers for three reasons:

1. Since they are low on the thinking "prestige" list in our culture they can lead you to innovative and overlooked solutions. (Tarzan had a well-developed sense of smell, but I am sure that no one would *expect* the same from a Nobel Prize winner.)
2. They are necessary for the solution of problems in which smell, sound, taste, and touch are involved (the design of a new hors d'oeuvre).
3. They augment visual imagery and each other to vastly increase the clarity of one's total imagery (more about this later).

Let us briefly discuss the first reason listed above. I often give my students problems having to do with developing devices to help blind people. I do this both because it proves highly motivating and requires ingenuity, and because it makes them think about various types of sensory inputs. Most of them attack the problem initially by imagining that they are blind. This is difficult to do, because sight is such an overwhelming input to most people that they find it hard to take the role of a blind person using their imagination alone. They especially find it hard if they generally think only verbally or mathematically.

After letting them work on the problem a while, I blindfold the students for an hour or two and let them wander about the world. This gives them, all at once, a chance to accept input from their other senses. They are then much more likely to use this very important data (to a blind person) to solve their problems. This simulation of blindness has limited accuracy, because when you are blindfolded for an hour or two your main problems have to do with walking, whereas blind people have long since overcome this. Still, the simulation is effective in bringing the awareness of messages from the other senses to people.

> **Exercise:** Try this experience yourself. Find someone to keep you out of trouble (not to physically guide you, just to keep you off the freeway, out of open manholes, poison oak, etc.), blindfold yourself, and walk around for an hour or so. You will be amazed at the sensory data you accumulate.

The second reason for using all the senses, "They are necessary for the solution of problems in which smell, sound, taste, and touch are involved," should be obvious. Just as an architect is better off with a good ability to image spaces and forms, so a cook is better off being able to image taste and smell.

The third point, "They augment visual imagery and each other," is more subtle. I am sure that most of you are aware that the senses augment each other. Food is a combination of taste, smell, and sight. Vichyssoise is as unsuccessful when one has a cold as an omelette is if it is dyed blue. An electrical storm needs sound as well as sight to be really dramatic. Sexual excitement benefits from feel, smell, and taste as well as sight and sound. Similarly, mental images need the full dimensionality of all the senses to be most effective.

In order to demonstrate this, I would like to give you another exercise. However, before you begin, I would like you to think of an apple. Got it? Now ask yourself enough questions about this apple that you can establish the clarity of your image.

I am now going to give you the transcription of a tape that Bob McKim and Bill Verplank use in a Stanford class in Visual Thinking. The tape is concerned with *clarity* and *control* of combined sensory imagery. It is played to small groups of students in an isolated and comfortable environment. They are typically sprawled comfortably on a soft, carpeted floor with no distractions present. They have been prepared for the tape by a talk explaining the serious purpose of the exercise and several weeks of class stressing the importance of sensory imagery.

**Exercise:**

1. Find a sympathetic narrator and preferably a few other people who are interested in this subject.
2. Obtain an outstanding apple for the narrator to give to each person.
3. Relax in a comfortable spot with the others.
4. Have the narrator read the following to you. He should read slowly, seriously, and soothingly, giving you plenty of time to fully establish the images before he goes on. You can help by giving a prearranged signal (a lifted finger?) when you have the image fully developed, at which point he can go on to the next statement.

"First close your eyes and relax. Direct your attention inward. Now imagine yourself in a familiar setting in which you would enjoy eating an apple. Relaxedly attend the sensory mood and detail of this place. Now, imagine that in your hand you have a delicious, crisp apple. Feel the apple's coolness, its weight, its firmness, its round volume, its waxy smoothness. Explore its stem. Visually examine details, see bruises, the way sunlight sparkles on the facets of the apple's form, the way the skin reflects a pattern of streaks and dots, many colors, not just one. Attend this image till your mouth waters. Now bite the apple. Hear its juicy snap, savor its texture, its flavor. Smell the apple's sweet fragrance. With a knife, slice the apple to see what's inside. As you continue to explore the apple in detail, return occasionally to the larger context, see your hand, feel the soft breeze, be aware of the three dimensionality of form and space.

"How was your apple this time? Probably a lot better. But your apple is probably still not as vivid as possible, simply because you don't really know what an apple is like. We've all eaten plenty of apples, but how often do we really pay attention. We are most often doing something else while eating, talking, reading, thinking, but never attending to every sensory detail. We're going to give each of you an apple now [hand out the apples] and you can eat it. We're going to ask that no one talk. All of your attention should be on the apple and on your sensations. Before you eat your apple, take a minute to examine it. Look at its shape, its volume, its color, its markings. Feel its temperature, its texture, its firmness, its mass. When you really know it, take a bite from it. Listen, smell, taste, feel, attend every sensory detail. Take your time.

"The apple that you have just eaten is now being assimilated by your digestive system. The apple is becoming you. Imagine that you are the apple that you have just eaten. Imagine that you are an apple on an apple tree. Take a deep breath. Let it out, and as you let it out, relax all tensions. Quiet all distracting thinking. Direct all of your attention, in a very relaxed way, to the pleasurable thought of being an apple on a real apple tree in a beautiful apple orchard way out in the country. You can feel the warm sun on your skin. You can feel a soft breeze. The sky is clear blue. The sun feels good as it radiates into your apple body. You can hear the leaves of your tree rustling in the breeze. You can smell the fragrance of the ripening apple orchard. It feels good to be part of nature. Now imagine that you are regressing in time. You are an apple that is going backward in time, becoming smaller, smaller, greener, tarter, smaller yet, you are evolving in reverse into an apple blossom. You are an apple blossom together with many other apple blossoms on your apple tree. You can smell the lush fragrance of apple blossoms. You can feel the warm sun on your delicate petals. You can hear the honey bees buzzing as they go about pollinating the orchard. In the distance you can hear a farmer's dog barking. You can taste your own sweet nectar. You can feel that you are an integral part of an incredibly complex natural process involving sun, earth, air, bees, the seasons. It feels good. Now you are becoming aware that you are more than a single apple blossom. You are an apple tree. Allow your imagination to move into the branch that supports the blossom. You can feel the sap that brings energy to the tree's leaves and blossoms. You can feel the sap moving through you. Follow this flow of energy down into the trunk of the apple tree. Feel the strength of the trunk in your own body. You must be strong to support branches loaded with ripe apples, and to resist the force of heavy wind. Feel the rough texture of your bark, the hardness of your wood. Now direct your attention down the trunk and into the roots of your apple tree. Reach out into the dark, damp soil. See the darkness. Smell the fragrance of the fertile soil. See the fat worms and the other subterranean creatures that work the earth. Feel the cool wetness and texture of the moist dirt and rocks, as your roots reach out for life-giving water and nutrients. Now leave the tree. Become the water itself in the damp orchard field. Feel yourself feeding the grasses and the wild flowers. You are part of a larger concept. You are essential to life. You are part of the much larger unity of nature. As water saturated in the orchard field, experience the sun's heat drawing you upward. Feel the sun evaporating your body, transforming your liquid nature into vaporous water. Feel your molecules rising upward into the blue sky toward the blazing sun. You and the others are now forming into a soft cloud. Down below you can see the earth, the tiny patch of the apple orchard, you are floating in the blue sky effortlessly. Quiet, billowy, incredibly free. In the distance a hawk is soaring. You are part of the creative cycles of nature. Now the sky is darkening, becoming cooler, you can feel the wind swirling and moving through your cloud. You are condensing with other molecules into droplets of rain. Falling downward, through the cold gray sky, downward, downward. You splash the leaves of a green apple tree and fall down to the ground, to the soil, to the roots, to the strong trunk, to the sap that feeds the branches, the leaves, the blossoms, the apple. You are the apple on the tree, in the orchard, on a rainy day. You can hear the rain splattering on the leaves, feel the cold stormy wind swaying the tree's branches, smell the rich odor of damp earth. Your apple, created by this marvelous interwoven working of nature, is inside you becoming you. And you, in turn, are a unique part of this creative unity. As you return now to your aliveness, here, and now, you feel good to be part of a unity which is inherently and eternally creative."

The students in the class do not use this tape until they have had quite a bit of experience in conceptualization, visualization, and imaging exercises of various sorts. However, we find that most people without this background are still able to build a crunchy luscious apple image in the first portion of the tape and enjoy their real apple with heightened sensory awareness. We find that people have more difficulty with the "control" portion of the tape and find it less relevant than the students do. However, it is useful as another indication of your ability to control imagery. You may now get a real apple, if you haven't already, and eat it as you proceed with the next section, which has to do with the difference in thinking styles among people. However, keep in mind that there are a very large number of problem-solving languages, some of which you use easily, some of which you are familiar with, and some which you may never encounter. You don't need to be expert at all of them, although creativity benefits from a larger vocabulary. However, to be uncomfortable with unfamiliar ones simply because they are strange is a definite inhibition to creativity.

## Cognitive Diversity

As well as thinking languages, there is the issue of cognitive (intellectual) style—the type of thinking we prefer to do. The following table lists adjectives that might be applied to the word *thinking*. These words also imply problem-solving styles or thinking specialities. The list is by no means complete; it is included to give you an indication of some types of specialties. The first column contains words that describe thinking

| *Strategic* | *Personality Related* | *Disciplinary* | *Overall Quality* | *Miscellaneous* |
|---|---|---|---|---|
| Inductive | Optimistic | Scientific | Quick | Visual |
| Deductive | Pessimistic | Humanistic | Slow | Wishful |
| Critical | Paranoid | Mathematical | Sloppy | Tough- |
| Intuitive | Neurotic | Verbal | Keen | minded |
| Analytic | Compulsive | Legal | Fuzzy | Literal |
| Imaginative | Obsessive | Medical | Clear | Expressive |
| Converging | Schizophrenic | Technological | Right | Exaggerated |
| Diverging | Twisted | Anthropological | Shallow | Random |
| Rational | Warped | Sociological | Deep | Instinctive |
| Irrational | Distorted | Historical | Methodical | Insightful |
| Forward | Pigheaded | Market-oriented | Plodding | Constructive |
| Backward | Wrong-headed | Product-oriented | Brilliant | Aesthetic |
| Focused | Stubborn | People-oriented | Mercurial | Creative |
| Narrow | Maudlin | Financial | Muddled | Efficient |
| Broad | Introverted | | Productive | Precise |
| Incisive | Extroverted | | Powerful | Innovative |
| Decisive | Weird | | | Practical |
| Indecisive | Sick | | | |
| Judgmental | Kinky | | | |
| Theoretical | Aggressive | | | |
| Applied | | | | |
| Additive | | | | |
| Eliminative | | | | |
| Qualitative | | | | |
| Quantitative | | | | |
| Objective | | | | |
| Subjective | | | | |

strategies and methods of attacking problems. The second column consists of words that are often used to describe thinking but which are obviously reflections on personality. Upon compiling this list, I was astounded by the number of words that have negative personality connotations. See if you can add some with positive connotations. The third column refers to disciplinary specializations. These are often related to the schooling we have had and the way we make our living. This column has the potential to be extremely long, of course, because we have all developed specializations that help us be proficient in our jobs. The fourth column contains words that refer to the overall quality of thinking. The last is a miscellaneous column.

As you read the words, notice which ones cause you positive or negative emotion. The positive ones are probably consistent with your preferred problem-solving styles. Which styles are consistent with being able to adapt to change and be creative? Which ones are consistent with the status quo? Which ones do you admire the most? Which ones would you like more of? Can you think of words that should be added to the list? Would you like to see some words deleted? Can you think of a better list format? See if you can list your own preferred and nonpreferred problem-solving specialties and those of your friends and the members of your household.

Intellectual specialization is valuable to us. Specialties are psychologically healthy. If you are extraordinarily good at something, you are likely to have a much healthier ego. A common example of this is the apparently fearless venturing of highly credentialled people (Nobel-prize winners, ex-presidents of large corporations, professional athletes, politicians) into areas for which they have little if any formal training or even competence. Specialties are also socially invaluable. It is simply not possible to maintain the complex social institutions we have without specialization. Organizations would obviously not be able to function as they do without people who have become extremely specialized and, therefore, proficient in their fields. Neither could our nations, our cities, our schools, or even our homes.

## The Problems of Specialization

But specialization has a down side as far as creativity is concerned. Intellectual specialities are sometimes described as "grooves" in the mind caused by repetition and reward. This is an old metaphor probably tracing back to William James and now a part of our vocabulary (the "grooved" swing). Unfortunately, a groove is not too far from a rut. Many of the problems I see are a result of people attempting to inflict their own preferred problem-solving style on others or on the world and/or not appreciating the value of other ones. A professional example can be seen in many companies in the interaction (or lack of) between the problem-solving styles of marketing and those of new product development. Both of these activities are necessary in a healthy company and, in fact, many companies get into trouble when one function tends to dominate at the wrong time. However, the specializations of the people involved tend to lead them into different philosophies. To product-development people, progress is improvement in the product itself, whether it be functional, visual, or economic. Their focus is internal, toward the company design, development, manufacturing capability, and pertinent technology.

Marketing people, on the other hand, have an outward focus. They are tuned to customer needs, which may not be consistent with technical progress. It is possible in a company to find the engineers attempting to develop a faster, more expensive printer and the marketing people calling for a slower, cheaper printer. Should this situation continue, great pain can result. Similar differences in attitude come from the relative specializations of product design and manufacturing people, managers and workers, hardware and software experts, research and product development people, first-line managers and middle managers, line and staff people, professors and students, teenagers and parents, and husbands and wives.

Broadening one's vocabulary of problem-solving styles is a good way to increase creativity. So is working with people of other problem-solving styles. Diversity in cognitive styles leads to greater creativity. It does not always lead to greater harmony and consensus, but neither are harmony and consensus always related to creativity. More about that later. Let us imagine that we could plot problem-solving styles of individuals in some way such as that shown in the figure below. There are two extreme ways in which such a group of people could operate. One would be at the overlap, making use of problem-solving specialties that are common to all members. This is not an uncommon way of operating and in certain situations gives great benefit. An unstructured group of peers will tend to

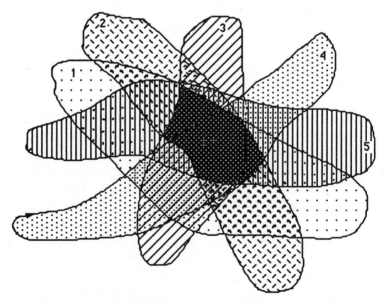

The Problem-Solving Styles of Five Individuals.

operate in this way. If you have ever played a game called Desert Survival (there are similar ones called Lunar Survival and Arctic Survival), your group probably operated in this way. In this game you are asked to imagine that you are stranded in a hostile place with a group of 15 objects. You are to rank the objects in order of usefulness. You first do it as individuals and then as a group. There are experts in these situations, and the group ranking is usually in closer agreement with the expert rankings than the individual rankings. There are obvious reasons for this. Groups operating in common problem-solving areas are wise, converging, and conservative. They are also smoothly running and quite happy. They are not good at creativity and change because the success of the group is due to its ability to suppress deviance from conventional wisdom.

The other extreme operating mode would be to use the envelope of all of the individual problem-solving styles. In this case, we have an intellectual capability that far surpasses that of any individuals in the group. The group is, if you will, smarter. It is capable of great creativity and change. However, it must be managed carefully because it will obviously be rife with discomfort, disagreement, and divergence. It is, however, a powerful resource and will not be guilty of "group think" if properly managed.

How can such a group come about? By expanding one's acceptable vocabulary of problem-solving styles, an individual can approach such a group. An existing group of people can be brought closer to this mode by encouragement and proper management. However, an even quicker way is through formation of an ad hoc group, a task force, a study team, or other assemblage of people with different intellectual preferences. Such a group begins with the desired variety of cognitive styles. We will discuss this in more detail in Chapters 8 and 9, which have to do with group and organizational creativity.

Let us talk about problem-solving specialties still more specifically in order to reinforce this message. We will discuss four specific sets of problem-solving styles or specialties in order to better illustrate what we mean. These four are typical of broad cognitive style differences that we encounter. There are many others, but if you have an understanding of these, you will be better able to think in terms of cognitive styles and be better equipped to find more productive ways of solving problems in groups.

## Analysis-Synthesis

Strictly speaking, the word *analysis* refers to the separation of the whole into its parts so as to discover the characteristics of these parts and their relationship to each other and to the whole. In this way, it is possible to develop an understanding of the behavior of the whole as a function of its parts. A clear demonstration of this can be seen in mathematics such as calculus where variables (the parts) are specifically defined and then worked with through equations to find the relationships between them. Analysis is widely used in science, literature, and all other fields. It is high-level human intellectual activity, and phrases such as "let's analyze this" and "analytical thinking" are everywhere.

Synthesis refers to the putting together of parts into a whole. The purpose of synthesis is to come up with a construct to satisfy the goal. An example of pure synthesis, if it exists, would be a painting by a child or the axe of very primitive man. I say "if it exists" because ordinarily even the most basic acts of synthesis are accompanied by some knowledge or rules based on analysis. The child has probably been shown that he or she should not move the brush toward the bristle end, and the primitive person probably analyzed the act of killing, defense, or construction that led to the concept of an axe.

To use analysis or synthesis alone penalizes us. It is possible to perform analysis as a pure intellectual activity (as in solving calculus equations), but the overall purpose of analysis by humans is to allow better synthesis. In analysis where unknowns and uncertainty are present, synthesis is necessary to adapt analytical techniques to the problem or, if necessary, to synthesize new analytical techniques. Synthesis is also benefited immeasurably by the use of analysis. Complex modern constructions such as large organizations, aircraft, sewage systems, or Christo's *Running Fence* could simply not be accomplished without analysis. It is, therefore, sad when those who identify themselves with the two problem solving approaches become antagonists. The painter and the applied mathematician, the poet and the chemist, the singer and the engineer should rely on a balance of analysis and synthesis, but they can often be found preaching the virtues of one to the exclusion of the other. This is always a loss, since the combination of the two is essential for creativity and reasonable change in complex situations.

## Convergence-Divergence

Convergent thinking focuses on an answer. Long division is a simple example, as is calculating your income tax. Techniques are used that eliminate uncertainty, simplify complexity, and enhance decision-making ability. Much of education is convergent. Certainly you expect the thinking of experts to be convergent. You would like your doctor to converge to a diagnosis, your architect to converge to a design, your auto mechanic to converge to a solution, and members of your family to converge to a few important problems for you to help them with. Techniques such as trigonometry, sentence-parsing, decision analysis, double-entry book-keeping, TV repair, and recipes for French bread are all convergent.

Divergent thinking refers to the process of generation of ideas, concepts, and approaches. It is an extremely powerful process and is perhaps less familiar because less emphasis is placed on it in our schools and public consciousness. It is possible to radically increase divergent thinking in problem solving. To the extent that more concepts are generated, decision making becomes more complicated. However, more alternates result in a greater probability of a better solution. Certainly more alternates are likely to permit a more creative solution, since initial concepts tend to be closely related to tradition.

Once again, the competent problem solver or problem-solving group should be able to handle both modes of thinking well and, in fact, in most problem-solving activities there is an overlap. It is inefficient merely to continue to generate ideas with no accompanying convergent thinking, as the pool will grow to a size that will make decision making nearly impossible. Similarly, it is foolish to converge without spending some effort to ensure that alternates have been at least examined, if not consciously generated. However, once again we find individuals, groups, and even organizations identifying only with the divergent (blue-sky, creative, idea person) or the convergent (tough-minded, decisive, practical). We find engineering schools obsessed with convergence and art schools obsessed with divergence, even though as a practitioner in one and at least a dabbler in the other, I do not find the difference in intellectual activities between the sculptor and the machine designer that great. As in the previous cases, separation by specialty is a loss, especially in situations requiring creativity and change.

## Deduction-Induction

Deduction and induction are another way of slicing the pie. Deduction has to do with reasoning from the general to the specific. It is usually associated with analysis, but this can be misleading. We use it to go from a theory to specific facts or from an equation to an answer. We use it a lot in school and when we are applying a technique. We expect that great detectives, such as Sherlock Holmes, use it because their overall knowledge is so scientific and complete that they can deduce the criminal in specific cases.

Induction, on the other hand, is reasoning from the specific to the general. It is the way that scientific theories are created and how we often solve problems. In most of life, adequate theory does not exist. We try to figure out the problem (and the answer) from observing specific shortcomings. Induction does not have as much mystique as deduction in our society because it does not seem as "right-answer" oriented as deduction. In that sense, it falls in with synthesis and divergent thinking. However, we rely upon it a great deal, especially in creativity and change. Competent problem solving requires both specializations.

## Jung and the Myers-Briggs Test

As a final set of specialties (this time more than two), let us look at the theories of Carl Jung, a contemporary of Freud's whose work is most easily understood by reading his book *Man and His Symbols*. He described people in terms of dichotomies of behavior. Four of these that are central to problem solving are introvert-extrovert, sensory-intuitive, thinking-feeling, and judgmental-perceptive. Introvert-extrovert refers to whether one would rather create and optimize solutions within one's own mind as an intellectual challenge (introvert) or whether one would rather solve problems and implement the solutions in the world (extrovert). The introvert is happiest wrestling with studies, enigmas, and complex situations that challenge his or her intellectual ability. The researcher is an example. The extrovert is happier organizing people and other resources to better accomplish results. The operations manager is a typical example.

Sensory people prefer to rely upon their senses to gather data—to observe, measure, read, ask experts. Intuitive people tend to rely upon information that is already in their memory. The sensory person may distrust his or her intuition if it conflicts with the "facts." The intuitive person distrusts the facts if they conflict with intuition. The thinking person prefers to make decisions by logically extrapolating from data, whatever its source. The feeling person prefers to rely upon his or her "gut" feelings and to make decisions according to emotional messages. The thinking person is likely to distrust feelings, and the feeling person tends to distrust facts and logic. A prospective house-buyer who is a thinker will probably not buy a house he or she loves if there is sufficient question about future housing values of neighborhood conditions. A house-buyer who is a feeling person will probably make the purchase.

The last dichotomy has to do with the judgmental style of the problem solver. One side represents the judgmental person who is sure of his or her stand (for example, the person who knows the relative value of nuclear energy and welfare). On the other side is the so-called "perceptive" person, who tends to adapt to the situation. Such a person is likely to be influenced by well-presented views of nuclear energy from opposing sides and to see both the good and the bad of welfare.

Problem solving requires all of these attributes. Certainly it is helpful to brood on problems within the mind in order to come up with more elegant and clever solutions. However, it is important to implement solutions if the problem-solving activity is to be meaningful. It is important to be sensitive to data as well as to the capability of the mind to integrate complex situations and respond with a "hunch." Analysis and respect for information is as essential in making good decisions as is sensitivity to the feelings of others and confidence in one's own course as evidenced through the emotions. Finally, judgment is necessary to come to conclusions, but a perceptive approach is valuable in being able to deal with options. Once again, representatives of the extremes often march under different flags. The assembly plant manager and the theoretical physicist, the technician performing experiments on an automobile engine and the painter following messages from within, the stock market analyst and the occasional Las Vegas gambler, the board chairman and the college sophomore certainly are stereotypes of different styles and probably would clash over values and problem-solving styles. They may not even get along very well. However, they each have something to contribute and to offer each other. The person who is strongly extrovert-sensory-thinking-judgmental certainly sounds like a left-brain thinker, might be expected to be an intellectual battering ram, and in fact is often found in management in traditional companies in traditional roles. The person who is introvert-intuitive-feeling-perceptive might be expected to be a right-brain thinker capable of a high degree of creativity and needing careful nurturing and support. To the extent that these styles do not come together, we lose important input, especially in situations involving creativity and change.

How would you rank yourself in the general population according to Jung's four dichotomies? Where do you think your spouse and children would rank you? How about your coworkers and your boss? These dichotomies are the foundation for the widely used Myers-Briggs Type Inventory. The test utilizes 126 questions to rank the test-taker in the population. The test, in turn, has become the basis of many popular books and articles.

In one of the summer executive programs run by the Stanford Graduate School of Business, participants were sent the Myers-Briggs test before the program. When they arrived, they received the usual large plastic name tag that contained not only their name, but also their Myers-Briggs score. They were then put in groups to work on problems and very rapidly learned to take account of the problem-solving style of others in the group. I do the same thing in my classes and have done the same thing with many kinds of professionals. Given a framework to emphasize and organize cognitive styles, people are smart enough to use them.

If you are in a problem-solving group that is running out of time to make a decision and someone in the group is overwhelmingly judgmental, you might be inclined to ask them their opinion. If you are interested in generating more options, you might ask that same person whether he would go buy some sandwiches for the group.

The figure shows Myers-Briggs scores for a number of executives with engineering backgrounds superimposed on curves for large sample populations. You can draw your own conclusions about this population. If it were the management of a single company, I would sure worry about the shortage of the "feeling" person. If I were trying to assemble a highly creative group from this population, I would certainly include at least one of the "feeling" people.

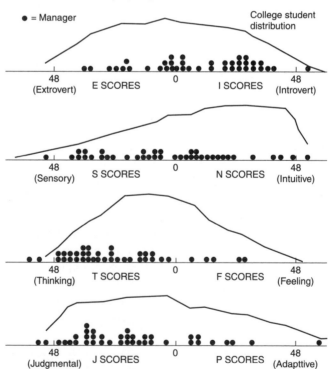

Myers-Briggs Type Inventory of managers with engineering backgrounds.

Using tests such as these to assemble creative groups has some risk. If one assumes that people on the "introvert, intuitive, feeling, adaptive" side of the test are more likely to produce ideas than those on the "extrovert, sensory, thinking, judgmental" side, one might lean in that direction in assembling the group. However, if one leans too far, the group might be too weak at convergence and implementation. Fortunately, in most situations, enough is known about the potential participants in a group to form one with not only a high level of the right kind of cognitive diversity, but with a low level of affective conflict—in other words a group of people who think differently but who do not develop negative feelings toward each other. The bottom line is that not to consider cognitive diversity in the formation of a group is to lose creative potential.

There are other problem-solving specialties, of course, and ways to measure many of them, although there is no universal instrument that can totally describe an individual, a group, or a large organization. However, for our purpose, we do not need the perfect instrument. We merely must keep in mind that humans are specialized and that these specialties can be described. To the extent that individuals, groups, or organizations cling too closely to a particular specialty, they fall into a rut, useful when the road is going where we wish to go and harmful when we wish to go elsewhere. To the extent that we are willing to take advantage of these specialties, we can combine them into new intellectual constructs, capable of increased creativity and responsiveness to change.

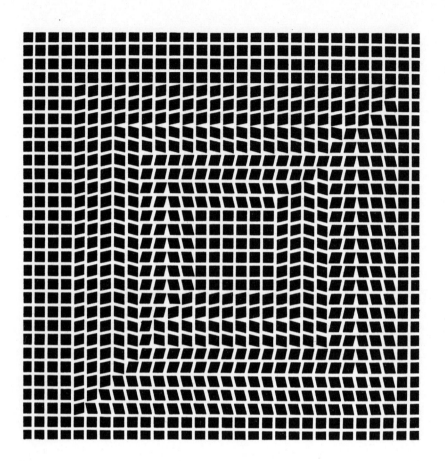

## CHAPTER SEVEN

# Kinds of Blockbusters

THE USE OF A RICH vocabulary of thinking languages and cognitive diversity, as discussed in Chapter Six, is one way to overcome conceptual blocks. However, there are many other methods. We will look at a variety of such techniques in this chapter. First we will explore a few techniques that allow the use of the conscious mind to overpower conceptual blocks. In a sense these techniques force thoughts that would not otherwise occur. The last part of the chapter will be concerned with methods to become more relaxed, less critical, and more intellectually playful during problem-solving.

The process of consciously *identifying* conceptual blocks takes one quite a distance toward *overpowering* them. Still, there are specific methods of going further. Many of these blocks exist because of the achievement-oriented, competitive, and compulsive nature of we westerners. However, this very combination of characteristics outfits us optimally for consciously overpowering such blocks. We think that people who are interested solely in good grades are often not as creative in school as they could be. However, if they are put in a course that is graded on creative output, they become much more creative. Their motivation and mental discipline are sufficient that they quickly figure out ways to become more creative and act accordingly. Let us talk about a few such methods that can be consciously applied to problem-solving.

## A Questioning Attitude

One of the most important capabilities in a creative person is a questioning attitude. Everyone has a questioning attitude as a small child, because of the need to assimilate an incredible amount of information in a few years. The knowledge that you acquire between the ages of 0 and 6, for instance, enormously exceeds what has been consciously taught. A great amount of knowledge is gained through observation and questioning. Unfortunately, as we grow older, many of us lose our questioning attitude. There are two principal reasons. The first is that we are discouraged from inquiry. After the child reaches a certain age, parents and others are often not as patient with questions (especially if they are busy and/or do not know the answer) that do not seem socially pertinent (Why can you see through glass? Why are leaves green?) and tend to discourage the questioner. Our educational institutions can barely convey the knowledge they are held responsible for (reading, writing, arithmetic, cultural lore). There is little time available for answering questions, so questions are effectively limited and discouraged. Many is the professor who begins his or her lecture with a plea for questions and then ends it with neither the time nor the encouraging attitude necessary to get them.

The second reason the child's "inquisitive" nature is socialized out of us (or at least diminished) has to do with "the great knowledge game." We learn as we grow older that it is good to be smart. Smartness is often associated with the amount of knowledge we possess. A question is an admission that we do not know or understand something. We therefore leave ourselves open to suspicion that we are not omniscient. Thus, we see the almost incredible ability of students to sit totally confused in a class in a university that costs thousands of dollars a year to attend and not ask questions. Thus, we find people at cocktail parties listening politely to conversations they do not understand, and people in highly technical fields accepting jargon they do not understand. One of my colleagues from my aerospace days used to delight in feeding nonsense jargon and erroneous arguments to people in other specialties. They would seldom question him in sufficient depth to find that he was faking. I have another friend who once successfully delivered a totally fraudulent hour-long lecture in aerospace medicine, of which he is totally ignorant, to an audience of university students. When his true credentials (none) were revealed to the students at the end of the lecture, they immediately voiced doubts that they had accumulated during the hour. They also registered extreme displeasure both toward the speaker and the instructor for violating their trust and wasting their time. However, during the talk itself, the competence and facts of the speaker were not questioned, probably because of the confidence with which he spoke and his extremely articulate lecturing style.

As I previously said, the questioning attitude is necessary in the broadest sense to motivate conceptualization. If you accept the status quo unquestioningly, you will have no reason to innovate. You will not be able to see needs and problems, and problem-sensitivity is one of the more important qualities of the creative person. Once the problem is sensed, the questioning attitude must be used continually to ensure a creative solution. A creative person should have a healthy skepticism about existing answers, techniques, and approaches.

In a fascinating book called *The Universal Traveler: A Soft-Systems Guide to Creativity, Problem-Solving, and the Process of Design,* the authors Don Koberg and Jim Bagnall discussed what they call "Constructive Discontent":

> Arrival at the age of 16 is usually all that is required for achieving half of this important attribute of creativity. It is unusual to find a "contented" young person; discontent goes with that time of life. To the young, everything needs improvement. . . . As we age, our discontent wanes; we learn from our society that "fault-finders" disturb the status quo of the normal, average "others." Squelch tactics are introduced. It becomes "good" not to "make waves" or "rock the boat" and to "let sleeping dogs lie" and "be seen but not heard." It is "good" to be invisible and enjoy your "autonomy." It is "bad" to be a problem-maker. And so everything is upside-down for creativity and its development. Thus, constructive attitudes are necessary for a dynamic condition; discontent is prerequisite to problem-solving. Combined, they define a primary quality of the creative problem-solver: a constantly developing Constructive Discontent.

This questioning attitude can be achieved by conscious effort. You merely need to start questioning. An emotional block is involved here, since you are apparently laying your ignorance out in the open. However, it is a block that will rapidly disappear once you discover the low degree of omniscience present in the human race. No one has all of the answers and the questioner, instead of appearing stupid, will often show his insight and reveal others to be not as bright as they thought. The most learned man can be overrun merely by continually applying the question "why?" or "how?" Pick a scientist, for instance, and ask him a "naive" question about something in his discipline. A few questions will drive him back through the basic knowledge which exists. Most of the questions you used to wonder about in your youth (What is beyond the farthest star? What is life? Why do people die?) are still unanswered.

In fact, the man who often is most admired at scholarly meetings is the penetrating questioner, who asks the apparently simple question that points out the flaws in a complex theorem or other structure of knowledge. Therefore, you have nothing to lose and a great deal to gain by questioning. The only thing you need to remember is that everyone is not as enlightened about knowledge as you (now) are, and some people will become unhappy if questioned to the degree that their omniscience becomes suspect. ("Why should man be creative?" "Because creativity allows self-actualization." "What good is self-actualization?" "It allows man to be happy." "What is happiness?" "Well-being." "What is well-being?" "Go to hell.")

If you still hesitate to ask questions, here are a few harmless and innocent questions. Ask them of anyone, and you will find that you are not as relatively ignorant as you thought.

1. Why do people sleep?
2. Do mirrors make letters appear backwards? If so—why do they not make them appear upside down?
3. A canary is standing on the bottom of a large sealed bottle that is placed on a scale. He takes off and flies around the inside of the bottle. What happens to the reading of the scale? What if he is a fish and the bottle is full of water?
4. What is licorice made out of? Why is it black?
5. Many cosmologists presently agree that the universe was created by a big "bang," or explosion, and that all of the stars are traveling outward from the original "bang." What preceded the "bang"?

**Exercise:** Questioning is especially important in problem-finding and problem-definition. You are going to use questioning in this manner. To play the game you need a cooperative person who is in a profession with which you are not very familiar. This exercise may take a reasonable amount of time, but if the person is a friend of yours or is interested in activities such as this, he should not object. Begin by asking him questions and ask them until you have a specific problem in his or her profession isolated and defined. Don't be satisfied with a vague, overly general, big-picture problem (medical care for the aged is inadequate). Try for a specific problem statement that is obviously soluble with a small amount of effort (for example, the sight of a novocaine needle scares people).

As you ask your questions, be aware of where your difficulties lie. Are certain types of questions (personal?) more difficult to ask than others? Can you observe the difficult period that results when you have used up your "social" questions and have to get down to work? What is your subject's response to different types of questions? Do you find it interesting to find out so rapidly about another profession (you should)? Were you able to go from a very general problem statement to a specific one? Did you work with several problem statements on the way to your final one?

## Working on the Right Problem

We are all familiar with our tendency to work on problems that we know how to solve or ones that are the most apparent rather than the core problems on which we should be concentrating. An oft-used adage is "if all you have is a hammer, everything looks like a nail." I would like to offer the alternate versions: "if you are good with a hammer, you prefer nails," and "if you see the nail most clearly, you grab your hammer." The skilled physician knows to look for the cause of the symptoms, rather than merely trying to get rid of the symptoms. So does the skilled problem-solver know to look for that core problem, which results in all of the other lesser (but perhaps more obvious) ones.

In his book *Stream Analysis,* Jerry Porras offers an interesting approach to finding the core problems in business. I have seen its effectiveness in business situations and have occasionally suggested it to individuals, with apparently positive results. Jerry asks his business clients to write out their problems on paper and then draw arrows between them showing which problems result in other problems. The figure on the following page taken from his book shows schematically how this might look. In actuality, if they are fairly sensitive to problems, a professional group can cover a very large area with problem statements in a fairly short time. Jerry describes problems such as (S3) in the figure as symptoms. They have many causes and attempts to solve them neither remove the causes nor the problems, since the forcing functions continue to exist. Problems such as (O1) are more profitable to solve, because they cause other problems. Problems such as (O3) are the most rewarding to solve, since they cause problems which in turn cause other problems. Want to try it?

> **Exercise:** Divide a piece of paper into four columns. Label one Work, one Material Goods, one Loved Ones, and one Miscellaneous. Write down your problems. Everything having to do with your profession, co-workers, boss, etc., goes into the Work column. Material goods includes those having to do with your house, apartment, physical possessions, economic situation, and so on. Loved Ones has to do with family problems.

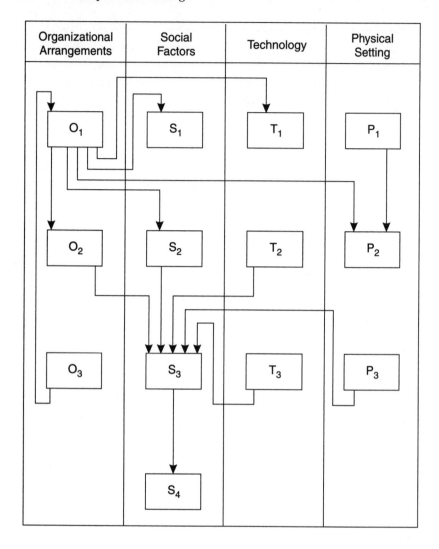

Miscellaneous is everything else, ranging from self-image to athlete's foot. When you run out of space, add more paper at the bottom and keep going.

When you run out of things to write down, draw arrows between all of the problems showing which is caused by others. All problems must have at least one arrow in (there is a cause for everything) and one out (your problems are at least making you unhappy). Then think about how consistent your allocation of energy is to the importance of these problems. Are you working on the core problems (lots of arrows out) or the symptoms (lots of arrows in)? Can you identify solvable core problems that would make many others on the sheet disappear? If you are convinced, pick a core problem or two and focus on them until they are solved. And then work on a couple more. Keep your sheet on the wall and watch your problems disappear!

## Time and Effort Focusers

Fluency and flexibility of thinking can also be attacked consciously. List-making is one of the simplest, most direct methods of increasing your conceptual ability. People often compile lists as *memory* aids (shopping lists, "to do" lists). However, lists are less frequently used as *thinking* aids. List-making is surprisingly powerful, as it utilizes the compulsive side of most of us in a way that makes us into extremely productive conceptualizers. It does not require (in fact would suffer from) changes in behavior and flourishes in a competitive environment.

Brainstorming, which we will discuss in Chapter 9, is a well known technique that involves list making with simple rules to ensure fluency and flexibility.

> **Exercise (Part I):** In order to give you a better feel for list-making, let me give you an exercise based on the "brick use" test attributed to J. P. Guilford. Imagine that you are a consultant for a brickyard that makes common red construction bricks and is in financial difficulties. The manager of the brickyard is interested in new uses for his products and has asked you to provide him with some. Spend a few minutes (three or four) thinking about the problem and then write down on a sheet of paper a new use for bricks.

Were you aware of what went on in your mind when you were thinking about the problem? You probably did some type of ad-hoc listing of alternatives. However, your conceptualization may have suffered from lack of focus, premature judgment (rejecting ideas that seem impractical), and labeling (choosing only the stereotyped usages).

> **Exercise (Part II):** Now take a blank piece of paper and spend four minutes listing *all* of the uses you can think of for bricks. Remember to aim for fluency and flexibility of thinking and not to get hooked into premature judgment or labeling. Make as long a list as you can. Go.

You may have noticed (especially if you did this exercise with others) that people tend to be very intense when listing ideas, particularly when a time limit is involved. This is perhaps a remnant from our educational system and the general competitive nature of our society. However, whatever the cause, listing focuses your conceptual energy in a rather efficient way and produces a written record of the output—both advantageous features. If the above exercise was successful, your "listing" effort should have gotten you much further conceptually than your original non-directed "spend a few minutes" effort. Were you fluent and flexible? As a calibration point in fluency, our design students average between 10 and 20 uses on this exercise. Some produce between 5 and 10, others between 10 and 20, and others between 20 and 30; a few produce under 5 or over 30 the first time through. The curve is roughly bell-shaped. *Fluency*, of course, is not enough in conceptualizing.

If your list were to consist of entries such as "build a wall, build a fireplace, build a patio floor, build a shoestore, build a hardware store, build a clothing store, build a grocery store," and so on, you could have been fluent, but of limited use to the brickyard owner who is probably already familiar with these uses. *Flexibility* of thought is also needed. You are flexible if your list included usages such as the storing of water, the warming of sheets on cold nights, the leveling of dirt, raw material for sculpture, playground blocks for children, and objects for a new track-and-field event (the brick-put). Such usages show an ability to see beyond the conventional role of bricks.

If you were doing this exercise with others, swap lists around and read them. Remember that some of the ideas should strike you as funny, if your flexibility is working well. If your list is lacking in flexibility, you may be suffering from the "premature labeling" block we discussed in Chapter Two. The usage of bricks is heavily stereotyped (construction material).

## Set Breakers

Many creativity "techniques" have to do with breaking our mental set—diverting us from accepting the answer that first occurs to us by making us develop and consider others.

In Chapter Two we discussed the listing of attributes as a method to escape the inhibiting effects of premature labeling. The listing of attrib-

utes is a powerful way to rapidly get more insight into the possible usefulness of an object, which in turn is an advantage in conceptualizing.

Let us list the attributes of a brick. Some of them are:

weight
color
rectangularity (sharp edges, flat faces)
porosity
strength
roughness
the capacity to store and conduct heat
poor capacity to conduct electricity
hardness

Think of more, if you can, and add to the list. How about economic
considerations? Aesthetic aspects? I am sure that you can now see that
by taking any attribute (weight), it becomes rather easy to list non-con-
ventional uses for a brick (anchor, ballast, doorstop, counterweight,
holding down tarpaulins or waste newspapers, as projectiles in wars,
riots, neighborhood rumbles, etc.). It is often a help in conceptualization to consider attributes instead of commonly used labels.

A clever use of attribute listing is contained in *The Universal Traveler* which authors Koberg and Bagnall call "Morphological Forced
Connections." They give the following rules for their "foolproof inven-
tion-finding scheme" along with an example showing how their scheme
works. Here it is:

### Morphological Forced Connections
1. List the attributes of the situation.
2. Below each attribute, place as many alternates as you can think of.
3. When completed, make many random runs through the alternates, picking up a different one from each column and assembling the combinations into entirely new forms of your original
   subject.

After all, inventions are merely new ways of combining old bits and
pieces.

*Example.*
Subject: Improve a ball-point pen.
*Attributes:*
Cylindrical   Plastic   Separate Cap   Steel   Cartridge, etc.

*Alternates:*

| | | | |
|---|---|---|---|
| Faceted | Metal | Attached Cap | No Cartridge |
| (Square) | Glass | (No Cap) | Permanent |
| Beaded | (Wood) | Retracts | (Paper Cartridge) |
| Sculptured | Paper | Cleaning Cap | Cartridge Made of Ink |

*Invention:* A Cube Pen; one corner writes, leaving six faces for ads, calendars, photos, etc.

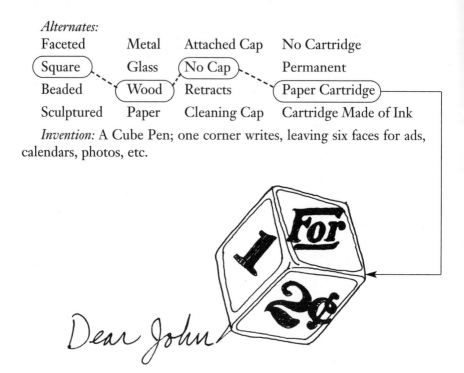

Another use of attribute listing, credited to Fritz Zwicky, is called morphological analysis. It is an automatic method of combining parameters into new combinations for the later review of the problem-solver. For instance, in an example done by John Arnold and taken from *Source Book for Creative Thinking* by Parnes and Harding, the problem is to provide a new concept in personal transportation. First of all, three parameters of importance are selected (more than three could be selected, but they could not easily be drawn on a piece of paper and put into this book). Alternate possibilities for the three chosen parameters (motive power source, type of passenger support, and the media in which the vehicle operates) are then listed on three orthogonal axes as shown on the next page.

If we consider each box on the figure we have generated, we find that it represents a particular combination of our three parameters. For instance, one represents a steam-driven system that runs on rails and has passengers in chairs. This is not so interesting because it is a train and has already been thought of. So has the system that is driven by elec-

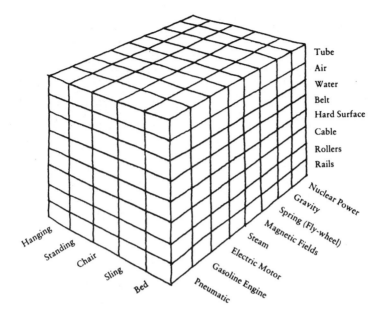

tricity and slings people from a cable (ski lift) and the gasoline engine powered one that seats people and travels on a hard surface. However, how about the pneumatic powered one in which people lie down and are transported through a tube, or the gravity powered one in which people stand and are transported down a belt? If one has access to a computer and can therefore consider large numbers of parameters, this technique can furnish enough combinations to keep the problem-solver well out of trouble as he sifts through them looking for something to spark an elegant solution to a problem. The creative "purist" would tend to scoff at this method as being too mechanistic. However, morphological analysis does, in fact, produce conceptual information.

Let me give you another example of the use of lists as thinking (rather than memory) aids. I am going to ask you to make a "bug list." People with a healthy fantasy life often play with the concept of inventing something the world needs and retiring on the proceeds. However, relatively few of them accomplish this. There are two factors that explain this lack of follow-through. The first is the difficulty in thinking of something specific that the world needs. The second is that it may require many years of apprehension, financial deprivation, and floundering family life before an invention can be made to pay off. The second factor is the more serious obstacle to this type of retirement. However, since it is not important unless the first hurdle can be cleared, and since we have no solutions here to the second aspect, let us pursue the first further.

In order to think of a potentially successful invention, it is necessary to establish a specific need. One way to establish or locate such a need is to interview people. For instance, you could go to the nearest hospital and start asking people on the staff what they needed. Another method is to play the role of a consumer group. Imagine you are a truck driver and see if you can think of something that you would need. A third, and perhaps simpler method, is to use yourself as the consumer. You must have needs that other people in the world share, and if you could identify such needs, you could invent something to satisfy them.

A problem that most people must cope with here is a tendency to generalize. If one of your needs is to eliminate air pollution or eliminate violence, you are setting yourself a tall task. (Better you have a need such as eliminating dog droppings from your front lawn.) The best way of starting on your retirement is probably to come up with a list of specific small-scale needs. A bug list is such a list. It contains as fluent and flexible and as specific and personal a list as possible of things that bug you.

> **Exercise:** Take a paper and pencil and construct such a list. Remember
> humor. If you run out of bugs before 10 minutes, you are either suffer-
> ing from a perceptual or emotional block or have life unusually under
> control. If you cannot think of any bugs, I would like to meet you.

On the next page is a list of bugs from a few present-day Stanford student lists. After you are done, see if your bugs are as flexible, specific, and personal as theirs. (You may also feel free to draw any conclusions you care to concerning students from this list on your own time.)

If properly done, your bug list should spark ideas in your mind for inventions. The list should ensure that specific areas of need are illuminated and that you have put in a reasonable amount of fluency and flexibility of thought. It should contain far-out bugs as well as common ones. For many of you, it may be the most specific thinking you have ever done about precisely what small details in life bother you.

After our students make such lists, we often ask them to turn them into inventions. Almost invariably, an interesting "invention" results. This requires first of all that the list be reduced to a few bugs of more than average potential. (Some preliminary thinking of solutions may occur here. Needs always seem to have more potential if a clever solution is available). Next we ask them to produce several concepts for the solution of each chosen bug. We then ask them to choose a concept and work it out in detail (including physical designs, where pertinent, and implementation plans). You may try this process if you would like. If you succeed and make a lot of money, send me some of it and I will use it for a charitable cause (my house payments).

## Bug List

TV dinners
buying a car
relatives
paperless toilets
men's fashions
rotten oranges
hair curlers in bed
hypodermic needles
  for shots
sweet potatoes
cleaning the oven
no urinals in home
  bathrooms
bumper stickers that
  cannot be removed
broken shoe-laces
ID cards that don't
  do the job
pictures that don't
  hang straight
ice cubes that are
  cloudy
glary paper
swing-out garage doors
dripping faucets
doors that swell and
  stick in damp
  weather
newspaper ink that
  rubs off
bikes parked in wrong
  place
lousy books
blunt pencils
burnt out light bulbs
panty hose
thermodynamics
dirty aquariums
noisy clocks

plastic flowers
instant breakfast
buttons which must
  be sewn
hangnails
small, yapping dogs
waste of throw-away
  cans
soft ice cream
crooked cue sticks
prize shows on TV
static charges—car,
  blankets, etc.
ditches for pipe that
  are dug too large
bathtubs
cigarettes
balls which have to
  be pumped up
changing from reg.
  to sunglasses
reading road map
  while driving
wobbly tables and
  chairs
big bunches of keys
shoe heels that wear out
campers that you can't
  see around
corks that break off in
  wine bottles
soap dishes that you
  can't get the soap
  out of
vending machines that
  take your money
  with no return
buzzing of electric
  shavers

pushbutton water taps
Presto logs
one sock
stamps that don't stick
chairs that won't slide
  on the floor
banana slugs
trying to get change
  out of pockets
red tape
smelly exhausts
high tuition
writing letters
strip mining
dull knives
conversion of farm
  land to homes
chlorine in swimming
  pools
polishing shoes
broken spokes
stripped threads
cold tea
X-rated movies that
  shouldn't be X-rated
bras
mowing lawns
locating books in
  library
miniature poodles
parents' deciding a
  kid's career
solicitors—telephone
  and door-to-door
portable computer
  batteries
shock absorbers that
  don't work
shaving

Another type of list is the "check list." This is a list that you can apply to the thinking process to make sure that you have not been trapped by blocks. John Arnold, founder of the Design Division at Stanford and one of the pioneers in design education, used a check list first put forth by Alex Osborn in his book *Applied Imagination*. It is reproduced below.

### Check List for New Ideas

*Put to other uses?*
New ways to use as is? Other uses if modified?

*Adapt?*
What else is like this? What other idea does this suggest? Does past offer a parallel? What could I copy? Whom could I emulate?

*Modify?*
New twist? Change meaning, color, motion, sound, odor, form, shape? Other changes?

*Magnify?*
What to add? More time? Greater frequency? Stronger? Higher? Longer? Thicker? Extra value? Plus ingredient? Duplicate? Multiply? Exaggerate?

*Minify?*
What to subtract? Smaller? Condensed? Miniature? Lower? Shorter? Lighter? Omit? Streamline? Split up? Understate?

*Substitute?*
Who else instead? What else instead? Other ingredient? Other material? Other process? Other power? Other place? Other approach? Other tone of voice?

*Rearrange?*
Interchange components? Other pattern? Other layout? Other sequence? Transpose cause and effect? Change pace? Change schedule?

*Reverse?*
Transpose positive and negative? How about opposites? Turn it backward? Turn it upside down? Reverse roles? Change shoes? Turn tables? Turn other cheek?

*Combine?*
How about a blend, an alloy, an assortment, an ensemble? Combine units? Combine purposes? Combine appeals? Combine ideas?

Professor Arnold had this check list put on a deck of cards, which he would ruffle through to see whether any of them would extend his thinking.

Koberg and Bagnall suggest in *The Universal Traveler* a list of what they call "manipulative" verbs—Osborn's original check list could be augmented by adding such words as:

| | | | |
|---|---|---|---|
| Multiply | Distort | Fluff-up | Extrude |
| Divide | Rotate | By-pass | Repel |
| Eliminate | Flatten | Add | Protect |
| Subdue | Squeeze | Subtract | Segregate |
| Invert | Complement | Lighten | Integrate |
| Separate | Submerge | Repeat | Symbolize |
| Transpose | Freeze | Thicken | Abstract |
| Unify | Soften | Stretch | Dissect, etc. |

Another type of check list is the one below, developed by George Polya of Stanford for use in solving single-answer mathematical problems. It first appeared in his book *How to Solve It.* This list not only exercises questioning ability, but also your fluency, flexibility, and originality through increased observation and association.

### Understanding the Problem

What is the unknown? What are the data? What is the condition? Is it possible to satisfy the condition? Is the condition sufficient to determine the unknown? Or is it insufficient? Or redundant? Or contradictory? Draw a figure. Introduce suitable notation. Separate the various parts of the condition. Can you write them down?

### Devising a Plan

Have you seen it before? Or have you seen the same problem in a slightly different form? Do you know a related problem? Do you know a theorem that could be useful? Look at the unknown! Try to think of a familiar problem having the same or a similar unknown.

Here is a problem related to yours and solved before. Could you use it? Could you use its results? Could you use its method? Should you introduce some auxiliary element in order to make its use possible? Could you restate the problem? Could you restate it still differently? Go back to definitions.

If you cannot solve the proposed problem try to solve first some related problem. Could you imagine a more accessible related problem? A more general problem? A more special problem? An analogous problem? Could you solve a part of the problem? Keep only a part of the condition, drop the other part; how far is the unknown then determined, how can it vary?

Could you derive something useful from the data? Could you think of other data appropriate to determine the unknown? Could you change the unknown or the data, or both, if necessary, so that the new unknown and the new data are nearer to each other? Did you use all the data? Did you use the whole condition? Have you taken into account all essential notions involved in the problem?

### Carrying Out the Plan

Carrying out your plan of the solution, check each step. Can you see clearly that the step is correct? Can you prove that it is correct?

### Examining the Solution Obtained

Can you check the result? Can you check the argument? Can you derive the result differently? Can you see it at a glance? Can you use the result of the method for some other problem?

List-making techniques can be used by anyone to assemble alternate concepts. They apply to the most rigid thinker as well as the most playful. They not only ensure good definition, but also that the ideas will last, since they are committed to paper. As we have already mentioned, ideas beget other ideas. If they are listed, they will lie around for days goading the idea-haver into other thoughts.

In a sense, such techniques as design notebooks, idea books, and problem journals are list-making techniques. A chronological record of a problem-solution is a list of all of the thoughts that have occurred during the solution of the problem. By its very existence, it causes the problem-solver to have more and increasingly imaginative concepts, especially if occasionally reviewed by others. We ask most of our students to keep design notebooks during their project work. These notebooks are complete chronological records of the thinking they have done and the information they have acquired. We collect them periodically for grading. We know that many of the students consider the notebooks to be an odious task and of questionable value and make most of their entries the night before we collect them. The impact this last minute "keeping up to date" has on their thinking is obvious. Groups that are apparently stuck on a problem will magically come up with new approaches the day that they hand in their notebooks. The intensive list-making they go through when padding up their notebook to meet our expectations is a powerful stimulus to conceptualization.

There are set-breakers other than lists, of course. Anything that breaks the usual context of thinking can function as a check list. George Prince, the co-founder of Synectics, was fond of opening a book, placing his finger upon the page without looking, and then trying to incorporate the word his finger hit upon into his thinking. Roger Von Oech, author of *Whack in the Side of the Head* and *Kick in the Seat of the Pants*, developed a deck of Tarot-like cards which he calls a Whack Pack. On each of them is inscribed something to do with your present state of thinking. Many of my friends have physical rituals ranging from running to golf that they claim break them out of their mental ruts. There are an increasing number of software programs intended to jog you in new directions in your problem solving.

"Conscious" blockbusters can be found in almost any "how to do it" book on creativity. Several of these are mentioned in the Reader's Guide at the end of the book. Many of them utilize some degree of list-making. Most of them include some gimmick to encourage playful thinking without the requirement of confronting playfulness head-on. Because of the difference in cognitive styles referred to in Chapter 6, some of these techniques are better suited to a particular individual than others. Effort is required to utilize them in a realistic problem-solving situation. The tendency of most teachers and authors (myself included) when trying to show the power of a technique is to include a sample problem which is a set-up for demonstrating it. Usually it is a simple problem that can be instantly solved if the technique is used and only with difficulty if it is not (e.g., visualization—the monk puzzle). The game becomes more difficult when you leave sample problems.

However, if you acquire sufficient practice with conscious blockbusters, they can be applied to complex "real" problems quite successfully. In fact, after sufficient usage, they will become second-nature. The specific listing of conceptual blocks is a conscious blockbusting technique. If specific examples are furnished, it is seemingly easy to gain an appreciation for these blocks. However, it is harder to identify them in one's own thinking, both because they are blocks and because one's thinking is usually more complex than the examples. However, if you put a good deal of conscious effort into looking for them, you will learn to identify them. You will learn what types of blocks to expect in various situations, aggressively search them out, and gleefully violate them.

## Using Other People's Ideas

One good way to break set is to interact with other people, especially if they think differently than you (an easy assignment, since everyone does). This is an especially powerful way of increasing creativity, since we have been brought up glorifying the independent individual creator and are conflicted about getting help with our problems. When reading history books, I am always fascinated with the fact that individuals (Gutenberg, Watt, McCormick, Edison) are given credit for new directions in technology. I suspect this is because of the desire of historians to reach simple conclusions and avoid becoming entangled in technology. If we look at contemporary developments (the computer, digital television, Prozac, the artificial hip joint) we have a little more trouble naming an individual who gets the credit, don't we? I am a believer that most significant human developments have been the work of many, and that if Edison had not been born we still would be enjoying electric lights. If one reads history books in non-western cultures, there is less tendency to give credit to an individual. One of the reasons for the disagreement over intellectual property rights between the U.S. and China is that the Chinese are not so sure that ideas belong to individuals. Therefore such problems as the "not invented here" syndrome (placing less value on something because you did not think of it) are not as significant. Think of the stigma placed upon copying. It took U.S. industry a long time to admit the benefits of "benchmarking" (keeping track of your competitor's products) and "backward engineering" (using solutions from your competitor's products). We sat for many years insulting the Japanese for doing such things as their products improved rapidly. Finally, for reasons of survival, industry had to admit that such things are good things to do.

As previously mentioned, cognitive diversity is a benefit to creativity. A good test for that is to ask for ideas on a problem you have from a large number of people including some who are not your friends. You will be surprised at the variety of responses you get, some of which you will find fascinating because they are so far from solutions you have considered. One of my most successful creativity techniques is to bounce ideas off of a group of people I know who think so differently than I do that they may be extra-terrestrials. (I don't want to ask them because they are so helpful to me that I don't want them to leave.)

This is not a suggestion that you break the laws of our country and end up in jail for patent infringement, espionage, or whatever. But you certainly can make more use of the cognitive styles and specialties around you. This is one of the reasons for the success of brainstorming. It is both free and pleasurable, since other people like showing off their brilliance in solving your problems (low risk compared to solving their own). In a corporation there are specialists who act as free consultants. Some people who do not think twice about asking advice from these specialists feel strange about asking for help from people outside of work. This is dumb. Life is hard enough without using all of the resources available to solve problems and it is not cheating to use other people's experience. There are few rules in improving one's creativity.

## Crossing Disciplines

Disciplines were mentioned in the discussion on specialization in the last chapter. They are worth a bit more attention here, however. As knowledge and intellectual approaches have increased, we have subdivided them into disciplines. We first meet them in school, where first spelling, arithmetic, and music are different, then English, algebra, languages, and social studies. If we go to college, we find that anthropology, sociology, and psychology are different and if we stay there long enough we find that cognitive psychology is a very different animal than behavioral. As a professor I live in a world where thermodynamics experts and dynamicists live in different intellectual camps, although undergraduates think they are both part of mechanical engineering and those not going to college could care less what they are at all.

Disciplines are accompanied by jargon, methodology, journals, and societies. Their benefit is that they promote depth of understanding, control the quality of work in their purview (sometimes unfortunately according to traditional standards), and provide satisfying tribal affiliation for their members. But, much creativity is now taking place between disciplines. I originally became a mechanical engineer because I did not like my electrical engineering classes—a not unusual way to pick a major in college. Now much creativity in mechanical engineering is through applying electrical engineering (integrated circuits, micro-miniature sensors and actuators, computers) to mechanical devices. Many breakthroughs in physics are through application of mathematics, in chemistry through application of physics, and in medicine through application of chemistry.

Discomfort in dealing with diverse disciplines, or at least people who are experts in these disciplines is a major block to creativity and often is based on long-obsolete experiences—bad teachers, dull books and old approaches. My advice is to try again. From observing students I get the impression that history becomes much more interesting as one ages. Just because you might have disliked history in high school or college doesn't mean you might not find it fascinating now. The same is true of many other fields.

## Crossing Cultures and Changing Environments

As mentioned in Chapter 4, there are great benefits from becoming knowledgeable of and comfortable with different cultures. Creativity demands both depth and breadth. Travel, living abroad, mixing with people from different parts of society is broadening. Trying to understand what computer experts are saying is both challenging and educational. If you are an elderly rich white male, attempting to understand the world as seen by a young poor black female can be a great help in social creativity. If you are a business person, attempting to understand people who are highly critical of business may increase your sales.

Changing environments is also an excellent creativity technique, but it must be done thoughtfully. I have attended many company offsite meetings, usually called retreats, and most of them could accomplish more. Companies will ship their people long distances to beautiful places and then schedule them inside a conference room full of communication equipment. They could just as well stay home. If you are trying to encourage people to bond, you need a common stressful experience not a conference room. The Marine Corps knows that. If you are an automobile supply company trying to get your engineers to think like Hewlett Packard Engineers, maybe you should try to convince Hewlett Packard to host your meeting at one of their plants and let some of their engineers attend so that they can learn about the automobile market. If you want people to think creatively the retreat should not be scheduled down to the minute. Environmental change must be tailored to the desired goal and level of creativity.

## Unconscious Blockbusting

In Chapter Three, we discussed the critical role played by the unconscious mind and its inhibition by the ego and superego. So far in this chapter, we have discussed techniques whereby you can consciously force your way through conceptual blocks. Through the use of various forms of listing and by consciously questioning and striving for fluency and flexibility of thought, it is possible to improve considerably your conceptual performance. These techniques work by utilizing the intellectual problem-solving capability of the conscious mind. In the remainder of this chapter, we will be concerned with decreasing the inhibiting effect of the ego and superego on the unconscious mind.

One of the most powerful techniques of enhancing your conceptual ability is the postponement of judgment mentioned in Chapter Four. The ego and superego suppress ideas by judging them to be somehow out of order as they try to work their way up to the conscious level. If this judging can be put aside for a while, many more ideas will live until they can be "seen." The dangers of premature judgment are alluded to in the following statement by Schiller (taken from a personal letter to a friend and contained in *The Basic Writings of Sigmund Freud*, edited by A. A. Brill).

> The reason for your complaint [about not being creative] lies, it seems to me, in the constraint which your intellect imposes upon your imagination. Here I will make an observation, and illustrate it by an allegory. Apparently, it is not good—and indeed it hinders the creative work of the mind—if the intellect examines too closely the ideas already pouring in, as it were, at the gates. Regarded in isolation, an idea may be quite insignificant, and venturesome in the extreme, but it may acquire importance from an idea which follows it; perhaps, in a certain collocation with other ideas, which may seem equally absurd, it may be capable of furnishing a very serviceable link. The intellect cannot judge all those ideas unless it can retain them until it has considered them in connection with these other ideas. In the case of a creative mind, it seems to me, the intellect has withdrawn its watchers from the gates, and the ideas rush in pell-mell, and only then does it review and inspect the multitude. You worthy critics, or whatever you may call yourselves, are ashamed or afraid of the momentary and passing madness which is found in all real creators, the longer or shorter duration of which distinguishes the thinking artist from the dreamer. Hence your complaints of unfruitfulness, for you reject too soon and discriminate too severely.

Delaying judgment does not come easily to most people, since we are taught to be severe critics of anything impractical, unrealistic, flippant, flawed, or socially frowned upon. Often we do not want to admit, even to ourselves, the existence of such thoughts in our mind. We certainly do not want to admit to others that we might think of roofing a building with feathers, of reducing air pollution by substituting sedan chairs for automobiles, or perhaps even of legalizing heroin to reduce crime. However, our minds should be able to conjure up these and much wilder ideas if we are to be truly creative thinkers. How, then, do we delay judgment? We can begin by using the conscious mind. Often if we can consciously make our ego relax a little, the success of the idea generation that follows may cause it to relax even further. We begin a game that is to some extent self-perpetuating. The easiest way to begin this game is to formally (by agreement with oneself or with others) establish a judgment-suspension session. Individually I may say to myself, "All right, I need some fresh ideas on this problem I am working on and I have a little time to spend, so I will suspend judgment and see what ideas I can think of. It doesn't matter if my thoughts are weird at times, since no one can see what I am up to." I am then free to conceptualize without judging the practicality of the ideas, since I am not imperiling my ego. After all, I officially announced to myself that I would undergo this activity and therefore it is not typical of my usual mental deportment.

Suspending judgment in groups can be even more effective than suspending it individually, since a spirit of enthusiasm can develop in the group and ideas may spark ideas in others. An extremely well-known technique for achieving this is brainstorming, which is described in detail in Chapter Eight. Another interesting technique that encourages suspension of judgment was developed in the early days of Synectics Inc. in Cambridge, Massachusetts. It is described in detail in *Synectics* by William J. J. Gordon.

This technique utilizes metaphor. Four types of operational mechanisms are used: Personal Analogy, Direct Analogy, Symbolic Analogy, and Fantasy Analogy. The *personal analogy* requires that the problem-solver identify with part or all of the problem and its solution. The *direct analogy* attempts to solve a problem by the direct application of parallel facts, knowledge, technology, or whatever. The *symbolic analogy* is somewhat like the personal analogy, except that the identification is between the problem and objective and impersonal objects or images. The *fantasy analogy* allows the problem-solver to use fantasy to solve the problem.

The best way of showing the use of the operational mechanisms is to quote a passage from Gordon's book. This is a so-called Synectics excursion between five people faced with the problem of inventing a vapor-proof closure for space suits. As this passage begins the group has just finished discussing the question, "How do we in our wildest fantasy desire the closure to operate?"

# Fantasy Analogy

G: Okay. That's over. Now what we need here is a crazy way to look at this mess. A real insane viewpoint . . . a whole new room with a viewpoint!

T: Let's imagine you could will the suit closed . . . and it would do just as you wanted by wishing . . . (Fantasy Analogy mechanism)

G: Wishing will make it so . . .

F: Ssh, Okay. Wish fulfillment. Childhood dream . . . you wish it closed, and invisible microbes, working for you, cross hands across the opening and *pull* it tight . . .

B: A zipper is kind of a mechanical bug (Direct Analogy mechanism). But not airtight . . . or strong enough . . .

G: How do we build a psychological model of "will-it-to-be-closed"?

R: What are you talking about?

B: He means if we could conceive of how "willing-it-to-be-closed" might happen in an actual model—then we . . .

R: There are two days left to produce a working model—and you guys are talking about childhood dreams! Let's make a list of all the ways there are of closing things.

F: I hate lists. It goes back to my childhood and buying groceries . . .

R: F, I can understand your oblique approach when we have time, but now, with this deadline . . . and you still talking about wish fulfillment.

G: All the crappy solutions in the world have been rationalized by deadlines.

T: Trained insects?

D: What?

B: You mean, train insects to close and open on orders? 1-2-3 Open! Hup! 1-2-3 Close!

F: Have two lines of insects, one on each side of the closure—on the order to close they all clasp hands . . . or fingers . . . or claws . . . whatever they have . . . and then closure closes tight . . .

G: I feel like a kind of Coast Guard Insect (Personal Analogy mechanism).

D: Don't mind me. Keep talking . . .

G: You know the story . . . worst storm of the winter—vessel on the rocks . . . can't use lifeboats . . . some impatient hero grabs the line in his teeth and swims out . . .

B: I get you. You've got an insect running up and down the closure, manipulating the little latches . . .

G: And I'm looking for a demon to do the closing for me. When I will it to be closed (Fantasy Analogy mechanism), Presto! It's closed!

B: Find the insect—he'd do the closing for you!

R: If you used a spider . . . he could spin a thread . . . and sew it up (Direct Analogy mechanism).

T: Spider makes thread . . . gives it to a flea . . . Little holes in the closure . . . flea runs in and out of the holes closing as he goes . . .

G: Okay. But those insects reflect a low order of power . . . When the Army tests this thing, they'll grab each lip in a vise one inch wide and they'll pull 150 pounds on it . . . Those idiot insects of yours will have to pull steel wires behind them in order . . . They'd have to stitch with steel. *Steel* (Symbolic Analogy mechanism).

B: I can see one way of doing that. Take the example of that insect pulling a thread up through the holes . . . You could do it mechanically . . . Same insect . . . put holes in like so . . . and twist a spring like this . . . through the holes all the way up to the damn closure . . . twist, twist, twist, . . . Oh, crap! It would take hours! And twist your damn arm off!

G: Don't give up yet. Maybe there's another way of stitching with steel . . .

B: Listen . . . I have a picture of another type of stitching . . . That spring of yours . . . take two of the . . . let's say you had a long demon that forced its way up . . . like this . . .

R: I see what he's driving at . . .

B: If that skinny demon were a wire, I could poke it up to where, if it got a start, it could pull the whole thing together . . . the springs would be pulled together closing the mouth . . . Just push it up . . . push—and it will pull the rubber lips together . . . Imbed the springs in rubber . . . and then you've got it stitched with steel!

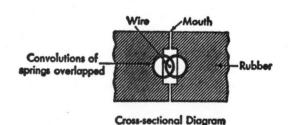

**Cross-sectional Diagram**

The Synectics technique results in a group of people delaying judgment in that they are willing to entertain ideas which normally they would probably reject as impractical. They can do so because the Synectics rules tell them to. They are effectively using a technique that, temporarily at least, relaxes the watchdog function of the ego and superego and lets the subconscious mind come forth with concepts. These techniques can be used individually as well as within a group, although the synthesis effect of the group will not enter into play. If you happen to think of using a brick as a hot water bottle, the realization that you are making use of the thermal capacity of the brick should quickly spark similar uses (bed warmer, warm floors, luau pit) in your mind just as it would in a group.

But what about ways to alter the ego's regulation of the unconscious mind without such techniques? Is it possible to somehow relax the control of the ego and superego in general, so that one may make better use of the unconscious mind? The answer is yes, but it is not simple. Let me try to explain the reasons for the difficulty by returning briefly to a discussion of psychology.

As mentioned previously, although there are many theories on the conceptual process to explain various characteristics of conceptualization, complete understanding does not exist. Many psychologists have attempted to explain the mental processes needed in creative thought and the motivations and characteristics of creative people.

## Maslow

Abraham Maslow was one of the more significant figures in the attempt to understand creativity. He preferred to talk about "primary" and "secondary" processes rather than about the unconscious and the conscious. Rather than referring to the primary mental process as the unconscious, he called it the "deeper" self, in the sense that it is hidden beneath the surface. Maslow also discussed primary and secondary creativity, as mentioned in Chapter Three. Secondary creativity is that which is evidenced by most people working in a system which requires a great amount of "discipline" work. It utilizes "right-handed" thinking and is based upon breakthroughs (primary creativity) made by others.

To Maslow, primary creativity comes from the deeper or primary self. It is common and universal in children, but in many adults is blocked off to a great extent. In an address called "Creativity in Self-Actualizing People" (contained in *Creativity and Its Cultivation*, edited by Harold Anderson), Maslow discussed a study he did of people who were especially creative and, as he puts it, "self-actualizing." He prefaces his discussion with the admission that very early he abandoned the notion that health, genius, talent, and productivity went together. Maslow found that a great number of people he studied were highly creative in terms of their own self-actualizing capacity, yet were neither particularly productive nor possessors of great "talent" or "genius." He was particularly struck by those people among his subjects who, though they had no noteworthy talent in any area conventionally associated with creativity, were in their daily lives original, novel, ingenious, and inventive. From this, Maslow says he learned to apply the word "creativeness" to many activities, processes, and attitudes other than the standard categories to which the quality is typically ascribed (such as literature, art, theories, etc.). Thus evolved Maslow's distinguishing between "special talent creativeness" (which is typically associated with creativity), and what he calls "self-actualizing creativeness" (primary creativity), which can be manifest in anything we do—in our most ordinary, mundane activities. In studying the traits of self-actualizing people who bring to their everyday affairs an attitude and manner of creativeness, Maslow located certain commonalities. He found these people to be more spontaneous, expressive, and natural and less controlled and inhibited in their behavior than the average. Their behavior seemed less blocked and less self-critical: "This ability to express ideas and impulses without strangulation and without fear of ridicule from others turned out to be an essential aspect of self-actualizing creativeness." Maslow found his subjects to be different from the average person in another way which he felt made creativity more likely: "Self-actualizing people are relatively unfrightened by the unknown, the mysterious, the puzzling, and often are positively attracted by it; i.e., selectively pick it out to puzzle over, to meditate on, and to be absorbed with."

Maslow saw a connection between *creativity in one's actions* and the *inner integration of one's self:* "To the extent that creativeness is constructive, synthesizing, unifying, and integrative, to that extent does it depend in part on the inner integration of the person." Maslow traces this to "the relative absence of fear" found in these subjects—both of others (what they would say, laugh at, demand) and especially of themselves (their insides, impulses, emotions, thoughts). "It was this approval and acceptance of their deeper selves that made it possible to perceive bravely the real nature of the world and also made their behavior more spontaneous (less controlled, less inhibited, less planned, less 'willed,' and designed). By contrast, average and neurotic people walled off, through fear, much that lay within themselves. They controlled, they inhibited, they repressed, and they suppressed. They disapproved of their deeper selves and expected that others did, too." By doing this, Maslow explains, the person "loses a great deal, too, for these depths are

also the source of all his joys, his ability to play, to love, to laugh, and, most important for us, to be creative."

## Barron

Frank Barron, another psychologist who did a great deal of research on creativity, took a slightly different approach. He was unwilling to accept overall psychological health as the criterion for a creative person, because he felt it necessary to formulate criteria which admitted to such creative talents as Beethoven, Hooke, Swift, Van Gogh, Rimbaud, Baudelaire, Bronte, Heine, Wagner, and others who created unhappiness. In an article in *Scientific American,* Barron stated:

> I would propose the following statements as descriptive of creative artists, and perhaps also of creative scientists:
>
> Creative people are especially observant, and they value accurate observation (telling themselves the truth) more than other people do.
>
> They often express part-truths, but this they do vividly; the part they express is the generally unrecognized; by displacement of accent and apparent disproportion in statement they seek to point to the usually unobserved.
>
> They see things as others do, but also as others do not.
>
> They are thus independent in their cognition, and they also value clearer cognition. They will suffer great personal pain to testify correctly.
>
> They are motivated to this value and to the exercise of this talent (independent, sharp observation) both for reasons of self-preservation and in the interest of human culture and its future.
>
> They are born with greater brain capacity; they have more ability to hold many ideas at once, and to compare more ideas with one another— hence to make a richer synthesis.
>
> In addition to unusual endowment in terms of cognitive ability, they are by constitution more vigorous and have available to them an exceptional fund of psychic and physical energy.
>
> Their universe is thus more complex, and in addition they usually lead more complex lives, seeking tension in the interest of the pleasure they obtain upon its discharge.
>
> They have more contact than most people do with the life of the unconscious, with fantasy, reverie, the world of imagination.

They have exceptionally broad and flexible awareness of themselves. The self is strongest when it can regress (admits primitive fantasies, naive ideas, tabooed impulses into consciousness and behavior), and yet return to a high degree of rationality and self-criticism. The creative person is both more primitive and more cultured, more destructive and more constructive, crazier and saner, than the average person.

Others have hypothesized other models of the creative person, ranging from the happy, well-balanced, suntanned, confident extrovert to the pain-riddled, warped, moody neurotic. Yet, the theme of unguarded unconscious (preconscious or primary self or whatever term we use) surfaces again and again. Therefore let us ask the question: What can we do to free the unconscious from its over-zealous warden?

Psychoanalysis might be an obvious thought, for it is intended to better integrate a personality by making the unconscious more conscious. It supposedly can ameliorate compulsive-obsessive behavior and therefore unlock the primary self. Many psychologists who have studied creativity agree that the goals of psychoanalysts, if reached, should enhance creativity. The fear that psychoanalysis will somehow "ruin" the creative powers of a person has been dismissed by most of the experts. However, for most people, psychoanalysis appears to be somewhat strong medicine for the improvement of creativity. It is expensive, it takes a long time, and its success is not predictable. Psychoanalysis may be attractive if one's behavior is such that life has become acutely unpleasant or unbearable. However, for "normal neurotics" it is perhaps overkill if we're interested in the enhancement of creativity.

## Other Paths for Freeing the Unconscious

Are there other ways to free the unconscious? Probably many. Maslow feels that any technique that increases self-knowledge should in principle increase creativity. In the cultures of the Middle and Far East there have existed for many hundreds of years what Robert Ornstein, in his book *The Psychology of Consciousness*, called "The Traditional Esoteric Psychologies." These have been concerned with personal, empirical approaches to self-knowledge, rather than with impersonal scientific approaches. These psychologies have often developed within disciplines such as Buddhism or Yoga and have utilized techniques such as meditation which are specifically designed to temporarily minimize linear logical thought and strengthen certain mental processes ascribed to the unconscious. Science is just beginning to understand "mystical experiences" and different "levels of consciousness." Ornstein believes that such experiences may be instances where the analytical left side of the brain relinquishes its usual control of consciousness and enables the right side to more freely interpret stimuli in a non-linear, non-deductive way. In his book, Ornstein makes a compelling argument for the integration of such psychologies and techniques with the "right-handed" psychology with which we are familiar. Certainly a higher degree of self-knowledge would result along with an increased respect for "left-handed" thinking. However, these techniques, as practiced in the Middle and Far East, take time and effort, and though they are currently becoming increasingly popular in the Western world, many of us are far from being able and/or willing to use them to improve our conceptual ability.

What paths are easily available to allow us right-handed Westerners to better free the unconscious? Maslow suggests education as one, and I, as an educator rather than a psychiatrist or mystic, must heartily agree. Maslow suspects that although education does little for relieving the repression of "instinct" and "forbidden impulses," it is quite effective in integrating the primary processes and conscious life. Knowledge about the psychological processes, about problem-solving, and especially about one's self can loosen the control of one's ego. The principle involved is a simple one: things are not as threatening when they are understood. Fears are lessened if their sources are understood, and most people's egos are "smart" enough to relax a bit if they are convinced that the results may be positive.

Understanding the workings of your mind is somewhat like understanding a golf swing. It allows you to work on changing your present actions in a detailed and conscious way. However, in the case of creative thinking, a side benefit is achieved in gaining a greater understanding of the workings of other people's minds as well. Many fears demand a comparison with other people for their maintenance. The fear of asking questions is often predicated on exposing your ignorance to others. The fear goes away when you realize that others are ignorant too. Similarly, you are less afraid of expressing your emotions when you learn that others have similar emotions, whether they have repressed them or not. Brainstorming works because the other people have silly ideas too. You are more willing to struggle with a problem when it is realized that few people consistently give birth to answers or solutions in a blinding flash of pure inspiration.

Therefore, I encourage you to read. The sport of thinking about thinking is an interesting one, and the literature to help you in this pastime is extensive. It can only lead to a better ability to use your own mind—a thorough knowledge of psychological theory and creativity research cannot help but increase your creativity. I feel that we have some effect on the creativity of our students merely by making a "big deal" out of creativity. By elevating it to the status of a class subject and by thus bringing it out of the underground, we cause our students to attach the same importance to it as they do to their other academic subjects and therefore to feel that they should, in fact, be more creative.

Many books and articles are available concerning the strengthening of one's self-esteem and self-confidence and freeing oneself from unnecessary fears and insecurities. The Reader's Guide section at the back outlines a number of starting points should you desire to journey further, with references to creativity research, psychological theory, and "self-therapy." The books on creativity research will give you a better overview of what is known about creative thinking and the characteristics of highly creative people. Psychological theory books will help you understand human behavior and how the mind works. The "self-therapy" books seek to apply psychological theory in a way in which you can affect your own behavior.

Reading, of course, is not the only way to gather knowledge about creativity and conceptualization. You may talk to psychologists and psychiatrists who are involved in trying to give people freer access to their unconscious mind. You may observe those about you and attempt to correlate their actions and their thought processes to their creative output. You may become more introspective about your own thinking (a must in any case) in an attempt to make it more creatively powerful and efficient.

One of the most important activities you should engage in is trying to free your unconscious to engage in creative thinking. If you brainstorm (or synect) or merely *consciously force yourself to be creative* (by use of lists or whatever), a strange thing happens. First of all, you usually find that if anything you are more successful in the world, rather than less (so some of your fears were groundless). You also find that creative thinking comes easier to you. There are psychological reasons for this. If you use your unconscious level, your consciousness gets the message that such activities are all right. This message is strongly reinforced if some of the outputs from the unconscious result in successes which the ego can revel in. The more creative thinking is done, the more natural and rewarding it becomes and the more the ego relaxes.

## CHAPTER EIGHT

# Groups

So far, we have considered only indirectly the effects of other people on individual thinking. However, much problem-solving takes place in group settings. We conceptualize with family members, friends, coworkers in community groups and volunteer committees, and with professional colleagues. In such situations we directly affect other people's conceptual process and they directly affect ours.

It should not surprise anyone that the conceptual process can suffer when many people are involved. "Group think" is hardly a phrase of acclaim; it implies blandness and lack of creativity. Most of us have heard the venerable definition of a camel as a "horse designed by a committee." But we must also realize that groups and organizations can excel in the conceptual process. Groups of people can bring many diverse perceptions and intellectual specialities to bear on a problem. They can provide a supportive emotional environment and the resources necessary to develop initial concepts into believable detail in a reasonable time.

During the past 15 years much attention has been paid to groups because of the realization that teams rather than individuals were perhaps the most powerful source of innovation in industry. The resulting research and discussion has resulted in a much clearer insight into the nature of the creative group, whether in industry or elsewhere. Some of the more important conceptual blocks that apply to groups are:

1. Inadequate knowledge of the creative process and use of group creativity techniques
2. Poor understanding of the roles of affiliation and ego needs
3. Poor leadership
4. Inadequate or unbalanced group membership
5. Lack of proper support

## The Process

I have been a leader of or consultant to creative groups often enough that I am frequently asked "how do you make a group more creative?" The technique that works the best for me is to get the members of the group interested in the creative process—the blocks and techniques outlined in the previous seven chapters. The people with whom I work are difficult to "trick" into being more creative, but are easily interested in the problem solving process. Once interested, they seem to have an internal motivation to demonstrate that they can rise above conceptual blocks. In fact, that is probably the reason that this book is still around. Who me? Perceptual blocks? I'll show you . . .

There are group techniques just as there are individual creativity techniques. Let us examine briefly two of these techniques. Perhaps the best known is brainstorming, a group problem-solving method given its name by Alex Osborn, the founder of the advertising firm of Batten, Barten, Durstine, and Osborn. Brainstorming groups generally consist of from five to ten people who work on a specific problem. According to Osborn, four main rules govern their behavior.

The first rule is that no evaluation of any kind is permitted. Osborn's explanation is that a judgmental attitude will cause the people in the group to be more concerned with defending ideas than with generating them. His second rule is that all participants be encouraged to think of the wildest ideas possible. His thinking here is that it is easier to tame down than to think up, and by encouraging wild ideas, internal judgment in the minds of the individual participants can be decreased. Third, Osborn encourages quantity of ideas, both because quantity also helps to control our internal evaluation and because he feels that quantity leads to quality. The final rule is that participants build upon or modify the ideas of others because, in his words, "combinations or modifications of previously suggested ideas often lead to new ideas that are superior to those that sparked them."

The brainstorming process benefits from having one member of the group act as a recorder, since a listing of the ideas as they are developed ensures that the group has continual access to its output and that ideas are not lost. The recording method should ideally be large enough in scale so that ideas are easily readable by everyone in the group. Brainstorming is most effective when the problem to be solved is simple and can be well defined. Brainstorming is useful at all levels of problem-solving, from the original attempt to formulate broad concepts to the final detailed definition.

There are a variety of behavioral reasons for brainstorming's success as a problem-solving technique. A study group at Harvard that investigated brainstorming in the 1950's listed these:

1. Less inhibition and defeatism: rapid fire of ideas presented by the group quickly explodes the myth that the individual often casts up that the problem overwhelms him, and that he can't think of a new and different solution.
2. Contagion of enthusiasm.
3. Development of competitive spirit; everyone wants to top the other's idea.

Still, delay of judgment is probably the most important factor that makes brainstorming work.

Brainstorming has at times received a bad name because it has been credited with generating ideas that are both shallow and in questionable taste. It has also been heavily spoofed and is sometimes identified with weirdness rather than thoughtfulness. However, the brainstorming process has some solid advantages and, if used when appropriate, can be extremely effective. A brainstorming group allows the pooling of a great diversity of background. Shallowness of output is often due to inadequate information available to the group and poor subsequent judgment, not to the technique. Brainstorming initially progresses rapidly when it attacks a problem because it is able to utilize common solutions. However, after these are used up, the process becomes more difficult because the members must come up with new concepts. It is in this later period that the technique has the most value. If the session is allowed to stop when the original rush of enthusiasm dies down (due to increased difficulty in thinking of ideas) it will not live up to its potential. The most effective way to learn more about brainstorming is to experience it.

> **Exercise:** Find a group of people and set up a brainstorming session on a problem that is easily stated in precise terms. Try to think of a problem that is important to all of you. If you cannot, try one of the following:
>
> 1. Invent some sort of function that would allow you to become friends with a few fascinating people whom you know of, but do not know personally.

2. Invent (in reasonable detail) a better way to divide a large (2,000 sq. ft. or so) room into smaller spaces which can be used by various groups. This is an ongoing problem in schools. The dividing system should be flexible (space sizes easily changed), cheap, and aesthetically pleasing.
3. Invent an astounding entrée for a far-out dinner party.
4. Invent a better way for handling road maps in a car.
5. Invent a Christmas greeting card you can mail to your friends that will impress them for all time and let you avoid mailing future cards.

## Synectics

Another group problem-solving technique is one developed by Synectics Inc. in Boston, Massachusetts.* It is more complex than brainstorming and more sophisticated in that it allows criticism and a higher level of technical expertise. Like brainstorming, it establishes the group's goal as problem-solving and thereby gives the participants the opportunity to satisfy their affiliation needs by solving the problem.

In this Synectics process the group works with a client who has a problem, giving the client ample opportunity to provide input to the group. The client originally states the problem and selects ideas from those presented. One particularly interesting feature of the Synectics process is that the leader does not contribute directly to the problem solution. The leader is a facilitator and a recorder and cannot contribute ideas of his or her own—the idea being that he/she is thus prevented from satisfying ego needs at the expense of the process.

The Synectics approach is particularly concerned with aiding corporations in the innovation process. In doing so, it relies upon a wide variety of principles and techniques. If a new concept is needed, Synectics uses an "excursion" such as the one shown here:

1. Leader asks client to select a directional Goal/Wish for which he/she'd like to develop Innovative Possible Solutions.
2. Leader picks a key word (action, concept) from the Goal/Wish.
3. Leader asks group (including client) to think of an example of that key word (action, concept) from a world that is distant from the

*The original Synectics group split into Synectics Educational Systems, headed by William J. J. Gordon, and Synectics Inc., under the direction of George M. Prince. The technique above was developed by Synectics Inc. (The technique described in Chapter Seven predates the split.)

world of the problem. The leader chooses the world. The leader then writes up a list of the group's examples.

4. Leader asks group to forget about the problem and the Goal/Wish and focus on any of the listed examples, thinking about its associations, images it conjures up, etc. Group members are asked to note these down on individual pads.

5. Leader asks group to use all or part of their example material to develop an Absurd Idea (probably impractical, impossible, or illegal) that addresses the original Goal/Wish.

6. Leader asks group to develop second generation ideas from any one of the Absurd Ideas (extracting key principles and applying them in a more realistic fashion without diluting the innovation).

7. Leader asks client to pick an idea that has appeal from the second generation ideas.

8. Process proceeds with paraphrase back to the original problem and itemized response from the client.

However, a large part of the energy in a Synectics session is devoted to the dynamics of the problem-solving group. The illustrations below

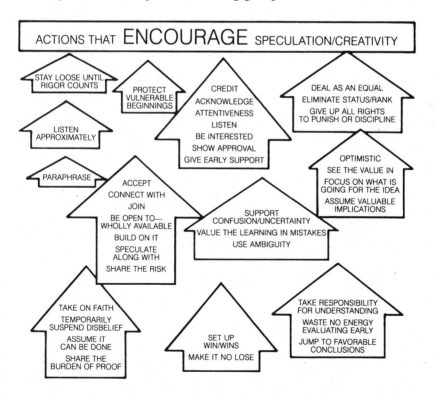

are taken from an article by George Prince, the founder of Synectics Inc., and shows the types of actions within a group that he feels encourage and discourage creativity.

The tone of a Synectics session is quite different from that of a brainstorming session. In the brainstorming process, ideas fly and the participants satisfy their belonging needs and their ego needs by seeing how many imaginative ideas they can produce. In Synectics, fewer ideas are produced and belonging and ego needs are satisfied through helping the client solve the problem. In fact, one of the traits a Synectics leader must acquire is the ability to deal gracefully with group members whose ideas are not selected.

An interesting technique incorporated into Synectics sessions is the use of an approach to evaluation in which negative statements must be preceded by at least two positive statements. The positives serve to give the group continual indication of the desires of the client. However, they also reinforce the originator of the idea and help maintain a psychological atmosphere which is conducive to creativity. The criticism

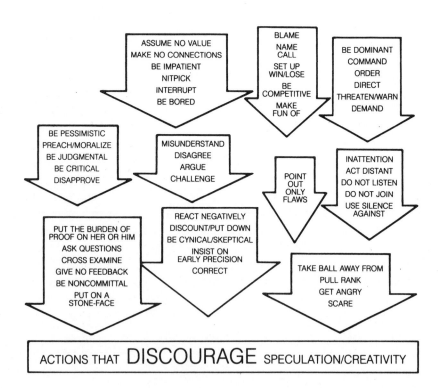

ACTIONS THAT DISCOURAGE SPECULATION/CREATIVITY

(the negative) is couched as a reservation rather than an overall no-vote and can immediately be made the problem for the next round. In this manner, rather strong criticism can be accommodated without inhibiting conceptualization.

Techniques such as brainstorming and Synectics are effective in group problem-solving because they deal with affiliation and ego needs in ways that decrease conceptual blocks. However, a group can accomplish the same ends without such formal techniques, providing it understands the factors that inhibit the conceptual process. Such knowledge is especially important in the leader(s), whether leadership be formal or informal, since a group leader is in a position either to support or squelch conceptualization. However, conceptualization will flow even more freely if all members share this knowledge.

## Affiliation/Ego Needs

In order to fulfill its function, a group must often operate like an individual. It must be able to find problems, think up possible solutions, and make decisions. It must also operate with a reasonable level of creativity: too much and it loses its stability, too little and it fails. However, a group or organization differs from an individual in that each concept, or action, causes a response within each individual member. It may elate some members, depress others, fill others with fear, and seem misguided to still others. A group or organization is in effect a minisociety which, in its need to operate as if it had a single mind, places great pressures upon its members.

Each member of a group or organization, being human, has strong affiliation and ego needs. Affiliation needs urge the individual to act so as to gain the social acclaim of the group: to be liked, respected, and valued. Many psychological experiments have shown the strength of these needs. In one classic experiment a researcher asked people in various groups to estimate which of three lines of different lengths was equal in length to a fourth line. Only one person in each group was a real experimental subject. The others were "shills" who had been instructed to reach erroneous conclusions. About one-third of the experimental subjects who went through this experience changed their initial correct judgment to agree with that of the "shills," even though the difference in line lengths was clearly discernible.

Another example of the strength of affiliation needs is provided in a passage in Professor Harold Leavitt's classic book *Managerial Psychology*. This passage asks you to assume that you are a member of a professional committee who arrives at a meeting with a strong position on the first item on the agenda. After some discussion, you become aware that the other members of the committee share an opinion that is very different from yours. Initially, the other members of the committee show interest in your position and honestly attempt to understand it. They also attempt to explain the validity of their stand to you, but you are sure of your position. As time goes by, the mood of the meeting begins to change. The other members grow impatient as they are unable to sway you to the majority viewpoint. You become aware that you are starting to be attacked, and your mouth begins to dry and your stomach tightens. They begin to accuse you of being hostile, of sticking to a position even though you cannot come up with "new" reasons, and of delaying discussion of more important matters by your reluctance to join the consensus. However, you feel that you must ethically stick to your point.

After an hour and a half of discussion, you are the focus of the group. All the other members are heatedly arguing with you and using everything they can think of to sway you, since this is a committee that likes to operate by consensus and you are keeping them from reaching the type of agreement they pride themselves on. Finally, one of the committee members turns to the chairman and proposes that the committee agree on the majority opinion and move on to other matters. At this point, you realize that you are to be suddenly cut out of the group, and in fact you are. The members turn their chairs and face back toward the chairman. As the chairman summarizes the reasoning for adopting the majority opinion, you occasionally protest points you consider absurd. However, except for occasional glares, you get no acknowledgment from the committee. You have been disaffiliated.

It is easy for most people to identify with the character in Leavitt's passage. It does not feel good. Most of us have had experiences with being psychologically rejected by a group of people we care about because we do not accept the common judgment. It is no wonder that people will accept wrong line-lengths and majority opinions which they consider wrong.

Affiliation needs underlie many of the conceptual blocks discussed in earlier chapters. People will like you if you think the way they do. But to the extent you succeed in aligning your thoughts with those of others, you can add to your perceptual and intellectual blocks. Problem-solving groups often become tightly knit and often consist of people who respect each other a great deal. Affiliation needs are particularly strong in such a situation, and severe emotional blocks can result. No one wants to fail in front of respected peers. A problem-solving group plays a strong role in creating its own subculture and environment. Blocks appear if these are not supportive to conceptualization. When a new concept deviates from the group's consensus, the originator may feel tempted to modify or swallow it. "Group think" can result.

However, when channeled positively, affiliation needs can result in high motivation (the desire for outstanding group performance) and a high degree of support. A group that understands the conceptual process can motivate individual members to think creatively, support them in doing so, and provide the atmosphere of trust that is vital if members are to conceptualize freely.

Ego needs at times may work at cross-purposes with affiliation needs. They urge an individual to influence others, to lead, to be significant, to be outstanding. Unfortunately, one of the easiest ways to be significant within a group is to be critical, but as we saw earlier, a critical approach can be highly detrimental to conceptualization.

Equally detrimental, however, are misdirected attempts, especially those of a leader (formal or informal), to influence others. Influence techniques that are the most satisfying to the ego are not always the most supportive to conceptualization. The use of authority, for example, is a classic Western method of influencing others, and it can be very gratifying to the person issuing orders. We have all experienced authority because it is widely used by parents. It has certain advantages: it is quick, and it requires a minimum of knowledge about those in subordinate positions.

The authoritative style of influence usually results in people's being told quite precisely what to do. Unfortunately, this can decrease the motivation to do anything else—a clear inhibition to creativity. Authoritative leaders tend to give their subordinates answers, not problems; in addition, they often inspire rebellion. A climate of mutiny is hardly ideal for maximizing the conceptual output of a person or group. Rather than overthrow the ruler, people can rebel by having no ideas at all. They can mentally "stop out," and cease to contribute productively and creatively.

By contrast, a collaborative style of influence can be relatively cumbersome, but it encourages conceptualization. Communication tends to be more informal; each member is encouraged and expected to contribute, and each feels a responsibility for the success of the group venture and therefore gains satisfaction of affiliation and ego needs from the problem-solving process.

Which approach do you think would elicit the best conceptual output from you, authority or collaboration? Since you are a thinking person (otherwise you would not be reading this book), you would probably choose collaboration, and you would be right. Unfortunately, since collaborative management techniques do not always satisfy the ego needs of managers as thoroughly as do authoritative techniques, they are often overlooked in our egocentric culture.

## Leadership

A few comments are in order about leadership. The classic authority-based, top-down, Type X leadership is not presently in vogue for innovative groups, yet there continue to be examples of revolutionary outputs from groups led in Atilla-the Hun style. What's going on? I sometimes divide groups into the following three categories:

1. Safe, compromising, wise, traditional group
2. Groups with an extraordinarily creative and dominant leader and supportive members
3. Integrated, synthesis-oriented collaboration with team-oriented leader

The first type of group is both extremely common and essential to the stability of our lives. In such a group extreme viewpoints are muted, there is little dissension, and conclusions are often by consensus. They are safe and wise because they tend to value the tried and true over the new and unproven. They are not especially creative, but in many problem-solving situations they are exactly what is needed. In these groups, the leader often has power either because of rank or because of expertise acquired in solving similar problems.

The second type of group can be highly creative. It is often found in company start-ups or in situations where success depends on a few unusually creative people. If you think of the outstanding people in any field, they often operate in this manner. But there is a downside to this type of group. It does not take full advantage of the creativity of the people in the group. Motivation to be creative is higher if one has significant ownership in the problem, rather than simply helping someone who calls all the shots and gets all of the glory. Dominant leaders do not necessarily help group members grow and develop to the point where they might find their dominance challenged. A group dependent on one person is also fragile. If that person leaves, the group may find that it is short a successor.

THE FLIGHT OF INTELLECT

*Portrait of* M.ʳ GOLIGHTLY,
*experimenting on Mess. Quick & Speed's new patent high pressure*
STEAM RIDING ROCKET.

The third type of group has many advantages, as could be expected from all of the buzz-words in its description. It operates as a team in which the members gain satisfaction not only from their individual performance, but from the accomplishments of the group. Personal and professional growth of the members tends to be higher and the output tends to reflect a wider variation of disciplines and cognitive styles. Finally, members of such a group are not only more highly motivated to solve the problem, but also to implement the solution.

This is not to say that leadership is not needed in such a group. In the 1970's and 80's there were many experiments with so-called leaderless groups that operated by consensus. One of the results of this consensus was often a leader, but the role of this informal leader was often confused because the group was supposed to be "leaderless." In addition this leader often did not have much clout outside of the group, and therefore was handicapped in securing support for the group. Leader or not, there were enough flaws in such groups that they are now seldom found. Groups involved in creative problem solving need a strong sense of direction and good political and economic interaction with the context in which they operate. In addition, groups benefit greatly if someone with good personal skills (the leader) plays the roles of referee and cheerleader. This is especially true if the group consists of independent people representing different disciplines and problem-solving styles, as is desirable in creative groups.

A good example of the importance of such leadership, or lack of same, can be seen in the type of university in which I have earned my paycheck. Most scholarly creativity takes place in faculty research groups which typically consist of a dominant professor aided and abetted by graduate students and perhaps professional aides. This is the traditional university model which assumes that the most important source of creativity is the individual. But times are changing. Much potentially exciting work involves a number of disciplines. New technology is altering the way in which information is stored and delivered. Student and public expectations are not the same as they used to be. A great deal of creativity is needed to augment the traditional model.

As a long-time professor, I am a staunch believer in the principle that the faculty of a school should make the decisions about academic directions. And at my school the faculty does this. Problems are typically addressed by groups of faculty members who either represent a discipline (research groups, divisions, departments, schools) or who are appointed to a standing or ad-hoc committee. However, these faculty members individually raise much of the money for their own activities, are focused on a narrow niche of their discipline, are quite allergic to being managed, and can easily move to other jobs, usually at a higher salary and with more perks. They are also leery about the effect of any change on their own activities. Consensus is usually sought for decisions, and the nominal chair often takes a relatively inactive role. The result is relative difficulty in exploring new directions involving interdisciplinary thinking and alternate ways of doing business. More leadership is needed to help all of these groups be a bit more adventurous, but the need is not acknowledged and the resources may not be available. The result is a great deal of inertia which slows exciting new directions. Universities are replete with the first two types of groups mentioned above. The third type is scarce.

## Group Membership

The make-up of creative groups is particularly important. One of the many books written on groups in the 1990's that seems to have good staying power is *The Wisdom of Teams* by Katzenback and Smith (Harvard Business School Press). In this book the authors list six basic elements for good teams. These are:

1. Small enough in number
2. Adequate in levels of complementary skills
3. Truly meaningful purpose
4. Specific goal or goals
5. Clear working approach
6. Sense of mutual accountability

A creative group should be big enough to represent the necessary disciplines and skills, but small enough so that the members can easily interact and contribute. In my mind, 5 to 10 is ideal. If large numbers of interests and disciplines must be represented, members should be chosen who are broad enough to represent several and they should be supported by specialists in the various pertinent areas. As has been mentioned, not only must the necessary intellectual skills be represented in the group, but also diversity of problem-solving styles and appropriate people skills. Bob Sutton, a friend of mine who studies organizations, is fond of saying that a creative group should have intellectual diversity but not affective conflict. In other words, they should disagree, but not fight.

As for people skills, those who are good in creative groups tend to respect and appreciate the thoughts and disciplines of others, have a good sense of their own competence, add to the ideas of others as well as submit their own, and have a sense of humor. Confidence is valuable, because it seems to help people work with new concepts and support others in the group. It is not necessary to be the ultimate brilliant extrovert. I have worked with many people who are extremely effective in creative groups, but who are quiet, unassuming, and even brusque. However, they have enthusiastically and selflessly contributed to the cause. Many extremely valuable people in groups are not the top people in their field. However, they know their field, their own limitations, and the people who are tops in their field. People who are bad news in creative groups tend to drag down the group through negativism, attempts to garner credit and control the group, and general divisiveness.

The other factors on the list have to do with the values and the experience of the individuals in the group. Hopefully, the group has a truly meaningful purpose, and if it feels it does not, it should certainly question its own existence. Similarly, it should have a specific goal or goals. In the case of creativity, the group should be responsible for ensuring that its goal/goals are stated in a way to be consistent with the amount of creativity desired. Similarly a clear working approach and mutual accountability are up to the group to establish. An edict from the leader concerning either will simply not result in the necessary buy-in from all group members.

It is certainly possible to improve one's effectiveness in a creative group, but it is necessary to encourage feedback from others and to practice the lessons that people have learned through studying groups. If one looks at fields interested in groups, such as organizational behavior, sociology, anthropology, and psychology, one finds a tremendous amount of material having to do with the way people interact in groups. Because of the complexity involved, there is no simple formula for the perfect creative group or the perfect creative group member. But there is great insight in these fields and it is well worth perusing.

## Proper Support

Groups need sufficient time, money, access to people, and support within the organization. In their book *Peopleware* (Dorset House), De Marco and Lister state that they do not know how to build the perfect group, but they know how to wreck one. Among ways to do this they list phony deadlines (the others have to do with managers who are afraid of risk or of a team that is smarter than they are, bureaucracy, physical separation of members, fragmentation of people's time, and reduction of goals). They maintain that sophisticated problem-solvers have a good idea of how long something will take, and will not seriously buy into a project that allows less. In Tracy Kidder's classic book *Soul of a New Machine*, the project managers solved this by hiring brand new graduates who didn't know how difficult the job was. But this can only be done in cases where brand new graduates have the necessary skills, and probably only once with a given set of people. The individuals and groups I know probably function better under some time pressure. But if there is not enough time to explore different paths in enough detail so that they can compete with past practice, creativity cannot flourish.

Similarly, money is important. It is important not only because it buys the necessary people and equipment, but also rightly or wrongly it is a measure of the importance of the project. Support for project initiation is particularly critical. As is well known, the initial funding for projects is often bootlegged by being charged to other efforts. This is necessary because people in charge of budget allocation want some sort of assurance that projects are feasible before they will fund them. If this bootlegging becomes difficult, creativity suffers. I have been part of two very creative organizations that have been the subject of congressional investigations, one because it did not succeed at an extremely difficult and unprecedented project as fast as some in government thought it should, and the other because it was suspected of misspending government funds (after much time and pain they were both found innocent). In each case the result was a drastically increased emphasis on accounting and auditing. This in turn caused increased difficulty in finding funds to try radical new ideas, and in my opinion, a decrease in creativity. Fortunately, time heals and political vendettas pass and creativity has returned to a high level in both of these organizations.

Access to people is critical. Not only do teams need members with the proper skills and experience, but they in turn must be able to tap the necessary expertise and thinking outside of the group. High mobility of people is often associated with creativity in an industry. It is one of the reasons used to explain the success of Silicon Valley. The job shifting typical of the younger technical work force causes rapid dissemination of ideas and skills. Individual companies may not like this, but the region and the industry benefits. Such people are extremely beneficial in creative teams. They often have the combination of experience and intellectual restlessness that is consistent with a high level of creativity.

Finally, support from the group context, whether it be a formal organization, or a more informal aggregation of people, is critical. This is a particular favorite of mine, because I seem to have a weakness for serving on groups whose conclusions are destined to be allowed to die. An example was a group convened by the then Governor of California and entitled the Governor's Commission on Toxic Waste. Since an election was in the wind and the incumbent's opponent was making an issue of the environment, it should have been obvious that this group was politically motivated. But California has a real toxic waste problem and this group was full of extremely bright, well-informed, accomplished, and politically powerful people. The leader was also a man I admired. The group also had great technical support from the University of California system and the members were quite bipartisan as far as political party was concernd. How could it lose? The reason, it could (and did), of course, was that upon realizing the severity of the problem, it recommended a number of measures that met opposition from the then conservative state government. They not only failed to support the group, but did a good job of suppressing the results.

We will talk more about the effect of organizations on groups and individuals in the next chapter.

## CHAPTER NINE

# Organizations

WE ARE DEPENDENT ON organizations. Many of us work in one, and it is in turn influenced by other business, governmental, legal, and financial organizations. Volunteer organizations often influence our lives, as do medical and educational ones. The cities we live in are organized, as are the stores and entertainment centers we patronize. In fact, any enterprise involving over twenty people had better be organized if it is to be effective. It would be quite difficult for an informal gathering of 10,000, 1,000, or even 100 people to solve a complicated problem quickly and economically. But the characteristics of an organization that allow large numbers of people to cooperate in accomplishing its goals can and often do inhibit creativity. Like individuals and groups, organizations suffer from conceptual blocks. It is worth looking at a few common ones. These are:

1. Too much or too little control
2. Age and size
3. Tradition and past success
4. Inappropriate reward system and support
5. Inhibitive culture

## Control vs. Creativity

Organizations control money, people, facilities, equipment, and other resources necessary to accomplish their goals. This control is necessary to allow large numbers of people to move in the same direction. But control inhibits divergence, spontaneity, experimentation, and therefore creativity. A major organizational problem is to properly balance creativity and control. Too much control and the organization may eventually become obsolete through lack of innovation and fail. Too little and it may fail through lack of focus and efficiency. This balance is a critical problem and too few organizations worry enough about it.

It is a complex problem because control in an organization is a function of many things including the output, the organizational function and level, the size, and the age. At present more product innovation is expected in the computer business than in the plumbing fixture business. If Intel Corporation were to focus merely on producing a cheaper version of a micro-processor rather than new and improved ones, it would not last very long. Neither would a company planning to sell radically improved bidets in Iowa. Within a given organization one also finds different amounts of control. People in internal audit are expected to be more concerned with it than those in advanced research. Control also varies with level in an organization. Some time ago, I conducted an unofficial experiment by calling people at different levels of the organizational chart at a large company and asking them whether they would like to hire extremely creative graduates who would pursue their own ideas even though they would bend the rules to find support and ignore advice to drop their project. People without management responsibility were enthusiastic. They would tell me how such an irreverent attitude is exactly what is needed to make something happen in a large organization. First level managers were a bit unsure. They liked the idea of the strong-headed entrepreneur, but were not sure they wanted to manage them. People in middle management were negative. A typical comment was "we've got too many ideas around here already. The last thing we need is people running in even more directions." People at the top were enthusiastic again. They were clear on the advantage of people who would start new ventures within the organization. Of course they assumed that the people below them had the details under control.

Let us consider age and size. Successful organizations seem to grow. Why? Large organizations have many advantages. One is their ability to make large impacts upon the world. Large businesses interact with large numbers of customers, make large amounts of money, and can have significant influence upon social institutions, governments, and individuals. Large universities can offer many programs and projects and focus sufficient resources to attain high quality. Large armies can overwhelm smaller ones, and large think tanks and architecture firms can often win contracts that smaller ones can not.

There is tremendous satisfaction in being involved in large-scale complex projects that involve a tremendous array of sophistication and interaction. One has only to spend time with someone involved in the design and construction of a large dam, ship, bridge, transportation system, or missile system to discover this. I was involved in the early days of the U.S. space effort and you do not want to ask me about it unless you have quite a bit of free time. It was large and I loved it.

Large organizations are also stable. One of the first modern organizational theorists, a German sociologist named Max Weber, coined the word *bureaucracy*. To him this was a word with very positive connotations. A bureaucracy was a wonderful, stable structure. Large, formal organizations in which jobs are tightly defined and control is rigorously exerted according to lines of hierarchy are relatively insensitive to the loss (or gain) of individuals. This, we must admit, is an advantage, albeit one that sounds somewhat inhuman and that we tend to take for granted.

They are also relatively stable in the face of changes in the market and during economic shifts. They tend to have a wider diversity in products and customers that protect them against changes in demand for a single product or by a single customer group. They have access to large amounts of capital and are able to exert political force when necessary (witness the famous government loan to Chrysler).

Large organizations also offer certain advantages to employees. They offer predictable paychecks and a high degree of job stability. This is once again taken for granted by many people. However, it is impressive to those who have been without regular paychecks. I found at one time in my career, when I was involved in hiring, that it was surprisingly easy to hire consultants into salaried positions. The freedom and glamour of a freelance existence often does not offset the wonder of a reliable paycheck. Large organizations also allow employees room to move and advance. It is possible to grow in one's career without sacrificing the specific knowledge one has obtained. In a similar fashion, large organizations provide a wide variety of mentors and opportunities to learn. They also offer prestige, especially to managers. (People are more impressed by the president of General Motors than the president of the consulting company that consists of me and my wife.)

Finally, growth itself is an advantage because it gives individuals more opportunity to increase the scale of their own operation and advance within a group or organization, lends excitement and a feeling of winning, and produces support from our growth-oriented culture. Have you been a member of an organization that voluntarily decided not to grow? They are rare, since most organizations can convince themselves that they could perform their work a bit better with a little more help. Even if the decision is made, no-growth is difficult to maintain because of its cost in morale. The university at which I work decided some time ago to not increase the size of the student body. This was a rational decision, because across the bay from this university is a very strong, very large competitor that happens to receive a large stipend from the state of California. We must be clever in competing with this university. If we try to duplicate it, we will fail, since lack of subsidy will cause us to market a similar product at a much higher cost. Our advantage lies in being smaller, swifter, and friendlier to our high-paying students. However, even though our student population is fixed (almost) and our faculty size is somewhat fixed, we continue to grow in facilities, outside-funded activities, nonteaching staff, numbers of transactions per month, acres of lawn and parking, and myriad activities. Growth brings improved capability and room for individuals to move. It also soothes the empire-builder dwelling within most of us.

## The Pattern of Growth

If growth and resulting bigness have all of these positive attributes, why are the advantages of smallness so much in the limelight? After all, most large companies were at one time small. They have grown for valid reasons. However, they have not grown without costs, and these costs have to do with our topic of creativity and change.

Structural formality inhibits communication and results in fiefdoms which can become protective of their turf. Free communication and the ability to combine activities in new ways are necessary for creativity. Perceived problems must be questioned, knowledge must be transmitted, and new and fragile concepts must first be brought to a state of reality and then sold to a conservative organization. Structural formality is usually accompanied by increased authoritarianism. In authoritative systems individuals attempt to perform well according to their job descriptions. But how many job descriptions contain the phrase "take risks"? Structural formality is also associated with routinizing, decreasing uncertainty, and increasing predictability. These may be healthy directions for business as usual, but not for creativity.

Large organizations necessarily devote a major amount of energy to control in order to be able to deal with the uncertainties inherent in complexity. It is not too difficult in any large organization to find people whose job is to prevent mistakes. Preventing mistakes involves reducing risk, which is also at odds with creativity. Because of this necessary control, the type of manager it attracts, and the more global responsibility of large organizations, they are conservative. An organization such as General Motors has far more difficulty betting itself on a new product, service, or direction than a small start-up. Large organizations are, by their very nature, resistant to new products, services, and directions.

They can also be depersonalizing, and here one runs directly into the motivational problem in creativity. Large numbers of people may be operating under extrinsic motivation, and rewards therefore become critical. Individuals and groups must be recognized for creative and innovative output. However, often in large organizations standardization of reward system dominates and the individual prospective innovator is lost. It is not uncommon for successful founders of companies to bemoan what they see as a loss of creativity in their now-large enterprises. It is instructive for them to compare the financial and psychological reward systems in effect during the start-up phases of their companies with those in effect during the mature phases.

Finally, large organizations can be too slow. The layers of procedure and control often are not consistent with the unpredictability of creativity. Resources are needed to allow creative developments. This is especially true in large organizations because concepts must be taken to a stage of development which will allow them to combat the conservatism endemic in the decision-making structure. They must be made available when and where they are needed. Lack of time, money, people, and facilities to pursue new concepts can paralyze creativity in any large organization.

The figure on the next page is from an article written by organizational behavior expert Larry Greiner. It details a process that will probably be familiar to you if you are or have ever been involved in any sort of organization. The figure is a qualitative plot of growth over time. By its upward slope it implies that successful organizations will grow.

The figure describes phases of growth in an organization and illuminates crises that the author feels are common. These crises occur at the ends of stable phases and may be abrupt or lengthy. They may or may not cause displacements in management and overall employment. Let us examine them and think about what they have to do with creativity and ability to respond to change.

The first phase on the curve represents the start-up. During this period the fledgling organization has a few to dozens of people, probably a unique product or service, very high motivation, pride of ownership and excitement among the employees, and informal and free communications. In the electronic business, this represents the revered "garage shop." Greiner calls it the creative phase because such an enterprise is capable of a high degree of day-to-day creativity. Constraints are

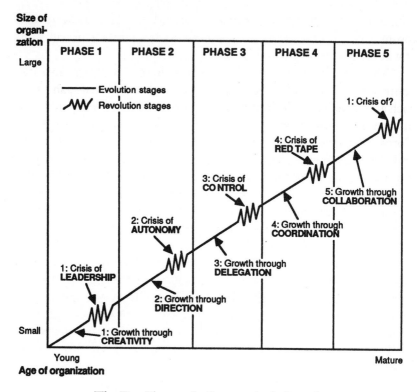

The Five Phases of a Corporation's Growth

few and precedent is lacking. The people involved are proud of the fact that they are blazing new paths and must be clever to survive. If a problem arises, they solve it, because they have no choice.

The first crisis (leadership) occurs when the organization becomes large enough (perhaps on the order of one hundred people) that it can no longer operate efficiently through completely informal organizational methods. It has hired many employees that do not have a sense of ownership, it is tying up too much of its resources in inventory, jobs are overlapping and difficult to describe to new employees, enough people are around that criticism meets most moves, and the enterprise is being heavily influenced by the IRS and various attorneys. At this stage, the founders of the company, even though they can read the handwriting on the wall, seem not to be reacting rapidly enough. In certain dire cases, they may not even want to read the handwriting on the wall. It is not unusual for management to resist increased formalization to the point where higher powers influence them or at least augment them with other individuals who are more formal in their organizational philosophy. If the organization is to continue to be successful, it will adapt. It will adopt a greater degree of control and formality.

Organizational charts, job descriptions, clear hierarchies, inventory control and accounting systems, production control systems, and other such accoutrements will appear. This is not to say that the organizations must take on the philosophies of the nineteenth-century British Marine Corps. Management may remain approachable and informal in style and should preserve as much of the motivation of the start-up as possible, but it must somehow simplify life for the members of what is becoming a mob. Some organizations have such dislike of the trappings of traditional large organizations that they choose to exert control through nontraditional means (corporate belief systems, pseudo family authority structures). However, with growth, more control becomes necessary. Control and communication systems become formalized in order to ensure that effort is not consumed in redundancy and contradictory decisions. The people-oriented chief may continue to leave the door open to all employees. However, a lower percentage of people walk through it.

The organization now does very well indeed with its new control-oriented habits and continues its growth. It may continue to think of itself as "small" even as it grows and acquires competition. However, eventually it runs into trouble again. It becomes increasingly cumbersome, because as size increases, the advantages of a strict linear hierarchy tend to be overcome by the complexity of its own communication and control procedures. People at the working level must simply wait too long for permission to act from the top. A point is reached where delegation is necessary. Decisions must be made lower in the organization and such organizational entities as profit centers, product-based groups, and geographically decentralized operating units must be established. Once again, Mr. Greiner predicts a crisis. Managers may not be eager for a change and may be pushed from above. Managers who direct an organization during the "direction" phase may prefer a life that appears tidy to them. However, if the organization is to remain healthy, a change will occur and the organization will enter the "delegation" phase.

There are other stages and other crises on the curve. The next crisis occurs at the point when the divisions of the organization have become so strong that upper management realizes that they could become independent units. The organization will then usually respond by taking advantage of possible synthesis. Companies will become concerned with coordination, company image, product balance, centralized policy, logos, product identity, and so on. The next crisis occurs when the organization has become so large that it is floundering in red tape, litigation, political forces, and general complexity. Those interested in more details should read the article. For our purposes here, we must only decide whether we think that there is truth in the article (I obviously think that it is of almost biblical stature) and, if so, what it has to do with creativity and change.

As the folklore suggests, creativity and responsiveness to change are more natural in small organizations than large formal ones. In the start-up, probably no one is even thinking specifically about creativity and change. The organization just does it, without self-consciousness. Its problem-solving habits include creativity and a high rate of change. However, as it grows, it becomes necessary to become more self-conscious and to adjust the organization to provide the environment for the desired creativity and responsiveness to change. In business, it is not uncommon for a start-up to be dominated by people who are oriented toward the development of a product or service. As the organization grows, emphasis necessarily shifts toward manufacturing the product more efficiently and selling it, since as competition enters, selling becomes more difficult and costs become a significant concern. At this point, the development of follow-up products and services often receives short shrift. At some point it becomes necessary to provide consciously for these activities. As organizational rewards shift toward those who control and cut costs, it is necessary to ensure that rewards for the development of new products and services do not stop. As resources move from product development to marketing to manufacturing, it is necessary to make sure that resources remain in product development and marketing. At a later phase, as delegation occurs, it becomes necessary to worry about whether time, effort, and rewards are made available to encourage creativity and response to change at the proper locations in the now more complex organization. It also becomes necessary to ensure that the proper people are involved and that the locations have the small and flexible nature that best encourages creativity and response to change. This often requires creating garage shops in the midst of a bureaucracy.

Examples of this can be seen in many highly creative companies. Historically the Lockheed Skunk Works and Bell Labs became famous for their creative output and contributions to the company. At present H.P. Labs and Xerox PARC are examples of such activities. These units must have the proper environment in which to function (support by upper management, adequate budget, proper location), be staffed with the right people, and be managed in the proper way. They must also be well integrated into the main organization in order to be successful. Many company research and development centers have been relatively ineffectual because they have become divorced from company realities. One of the reasons for the success of the Lockheed Skunk Works above and beyond its technical capability was that Kelly Johnson, its long-time director, had been a Vice President of the company, knew the culture and politics in the company, and was buddies with the other top managers.

## Tradition and Past Success

One of the most difficult challenges to continued creativity within an organization is past success. Many of you probably remember the shock in the 1960's and 1970's as the U.S. was jarred from its post-WWII complacency by Japanese Industry. We had emerged from the war as the supreme industrial power in the world. Many of our competitors (Germany and Japan) had been virtually destroyed while our G.N.P. had tripled. We became so confident of our innate industrial superiority that we could hardly believe it when basic U.S industries such as shipbuilding and raw-steel production lost their ability to compete, followed by optical equipment, consumer electronics, and even to some extent automobiles and machine tools. It took many years of looking for scapegoats (low labor costs, unfair trade practices) before we finally admitted that U.S. industry was lagging in innovation. We had become so successful that we simply could not believe that anyone could beat us. Part of the problem of U.S. industry was that its strength in product design had caused it to ignore creativity in production. U.S. companies often had developed products first (tape recorders, computers) but were simply beaten in the factory.

Another example of complacency in the 1970's and 80's was the neglect of creativity in marketing in many technology-based companies. They were so successful at devising miraculous products that they forgot that people had to want them. Realization came when some companies achieved outstanding success through learning more about their customers and employing sophisticated marketing techniques. We now see such things as the creative, successful and obviously expensive advertising programs of Intel, a company that initially sold their technically esoteric products solely by stressing cost and performance to computer manufacturers. Another example is the re-emphasis on invention in the advertisements of Hewlett Packard, a company that has always been highly inventive but perhaps allowed the public to forget that fact midst the flurry of attention paid to start-ups.

A final example can be seen from the many companies who fail to keep up with technology. In his book *Innovation*, Richard Foster discusses this. The illustration from this book (below) is a plot of performance vs. investment for four types of tire cord. The curve for cotton, the first material used in tire cord, is flat because its performance level was arbitrarily fixed at one on the chart. The other curves are more typical for technological products. An initial investment is necessary to develop the product. Subsequent investments improve the performance. However, eventually a point is reached where the curve flattens because there is less potential in the technology. Rayon displaced cotton because it was stronger and did not rot, and during the course of its lifetime some 100 million dollars was spent on improving its performance. However, as the curve shows, this was a game of diminishing returns. Du Pont and a company named American Viscose were the major producers of this rayon cord. Du Pont, however, switched to its proprietary Nylon, and as the curve shows, although the initial investment was much higher, the performance exceeded that of rayon. American Viscose lost out in the same way as the original makers of cotton cord. Polyester then entered

From Cotton to Rayon to Nylon to Polyester

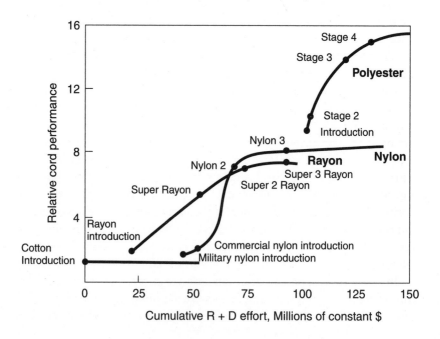

Cumulative R + D effort, Millions of constant $

the game, and once again, although initial investment was higher, the potential performance was greater. Du Pont was involved in this development as well as Celanese and other companies. However, eventually Celanese became the largest producer of polyester cord. Foster hypothesizes that this is because Du Pont had a vested interest in Nylon. In any case Du Pont lost their lead from staying with an old technology just as the cotton cord manufacturers and American Viscose had before.

## Reward System and Support

All of us, no matter how accomplished and independent, are affected by rewards, so it is not surprising that reward systems play a large role in organizational creativity. I have been a consultant to a large number of companies whose upper managers seemed to want to increase innovation. Upon talking to the people lower down in the organizational chart, I have often come to the conclusion that one does better in the company if one simply carries out orders and avoids rocking the boat. Bob Sutton, an organizational behavior professor at Stanford, is fond of saying that non-innovative companies reward success, punish failure, and accept inaction. Innovative companies reward both success and failure (assuming it follows a valiant attempt) and punish inaction.

Psychologists often divide rewards into intrinsic (internal) and extrinsic (from without). Both are important to creativity. The importance of intrinsic reward becomes obvious when one considers the many people who have caused changes despite adversity. Think of Ghandi, Martin Luther King, Nelson Mandela, and Jesus. Consider the artists who are "discovered" after their death. Work done by Teresa Amabile, a psychologist now on the faculty at the Harvard Business School, shows that in many cases intrinsic reward is primary. In her excellent (though technical) book entitled *The Social Psychology of Creativity*, she summarizes experiments that she has conducted with children and adults on creative tasks such as collage, storytelling, poetry, and cartoon captioning. She found that her subjects were most creative when motivated intrinsically. Extrinsic motivation factors (evaluation, peer observation, and rewards based on the quality of the output) decreased creativity. In her book, she supports her experimental conclusions with a myriad of references.

In one typical experiment, collages were constructed by 95 students enrolled in an introductory psychology course at Stanford University. They were not artists and had no significant previous experience in collage work. The collage was to convey the feeling of "silliness." The results were evaluated by fifteen artists who were shown to agree quite closely on their ratings.

The subjects were randomly divided into eight groups. Those in three of the groups were told that the only thing of interest was their mood and that the design itself was unimportant (no expectation of evaluation nor external motivation). The subjects in the first group were given no further focus, those in the second were asked to concentrate upon "technical goodness," and those in the third to concentrate upon creativity.

The subjects in the other five groups were told that the design would be evaluated by a panel of artists and that the quality of their collage would be part of the experimental data (evaluation expectation and external motivation). Once again those in the first group were given no further focus and those in the second were told that the judges would base their evaluation on "technical goodness." Those in the third group were told that they would be evaluated on how good their collages were technically, but were in addition given six detailed technical elements that the judges would consider. The subjects in the fourth group were told that the judges would base their evaluation on how creative the designs were, and those in the fifth group were not only told they would be evaluated on creativity, but were given seven specific criteria that the judges would consider.

The chart opposite shows the mean creativity for the collages assembled by the various groups. There was a major difference in the two groups that were given no focus. The subjects that were not expecting evaluation (intrinsic motivation) averaged much higher in creativity. The same is true of the three with the technical focus. Clearly, evaluation expectation also degraded the creativity of the subjects who were simply asked to focus on creativity. However, interestingly enough, those told the seven specific creativity criteria were judged to be the most creative of all.

As I have said, I believe strongly in the benefits of widespread knowledge of the problem-solving process in groups and organizations. To me the last column of the chart is evidence for this. Teresa Amabile explains the unusual creativity of those in this column (who were given the specific creativity "instructions") as follows:

"For two reasons, this high creativity of the specific creativity instructions group must be interpreted cautiously. On a practical level, it is unlikely that creativity in everyday performance could be enhanced by

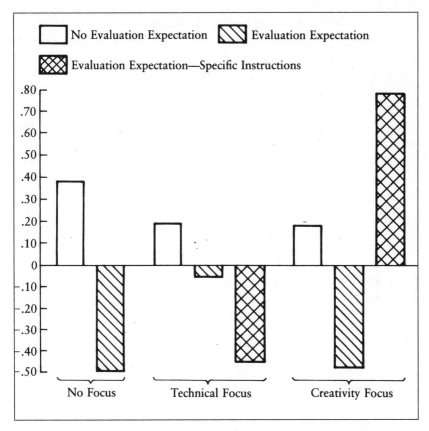

telling people exactly what constitutes a creative performance. The reason we value creative work so highly is that we cannot know beforehand just how to achieve a novel and appropriate response. On a theoretical level, the conceptual definition of creativity clearly disallows the consideration of the specific instructions task as 'creative.' According to that definition, the task must be heuristic (no right answer or known technique to obtain the answer) in order for the product of task engagement to be considered creative. In this study, specific instructions on how to make a collage that would be judged as 'creative' rendered the task algorithmic. Thus, according to the conceptual definition, it is simply inappropriate to assign the label 'creative' to the performance of the specific instructions group."

I agree with her interpretation in the case of highly original concepts in individual work. But how about more pragmatic situations where many people are involved and the results must be sold to the world, the typical state of groups and organizations? In such situations it seems reasonable to me that people with a more specific understanding of creativity and its characteristics would produce outputs which would be judged to be more creative. Most of us are not Leonardo, Mozart, or Einstein and perform better in a game if we know the rules.

Research such as this underlines the critical influence of evaluation and judgment in creativity. I spent some time as an art student, have taught many courses in design, and am impressed with teachers who can handle evaluation well. The challenge is to give students enough freedom and encouragement that they will explore, but also enough evaluation and feedback so that they will learn. Once again the right balance of creativity and control.

Since creativity seems to respond to intrinsic reward, to situations in which we are motivated by our interest in and fascination with the task, organizations seeking more innovation should take special effort to match people to tasks which they will be motivated to do through interest and personal satisfaction. This argues for mobility in organizations so that people can move as they learn more about tasks they prefer. Innovative organizations support such moves as a long-term strengthening. Managers who block such moves for selfish reasons are blocking increased creativity.

Can we rely totally upon intrinsic rewards to ensure creativity in an organization? There are several reasons why we cannot. One problem is that such an approach is counter to some traditional values in organizations. We think in terms of assigning people to work that needs to be done, not necessarily work which best matches their interests. The protestant ethic also suggests to us that perhaps work should be of a nature that requires external reward. As my father used to say, "If work was fun, somebody would do it for free." Another shortcoming is that even given activities that are so pleasurable that motivation is intrinsic, most of us do not have doors that are entirely clear of wolves. The people I know, for better or worse, are old friends with external motivation in life. I myself am a good example. In general I consider myself extremely fortunate in that I am involved in activities which bring great satisfaction to me. However, the activities which bring me pleasure are more complex than collage-making. I have not yet found a way to escape the short-term drudgery and trauma which accompany my long-term satisfaction. I am therefore continually fighting against my schedule and the clock to finish activities which are not as much fun to me as alternates I can think of (my hobbies, reading trashy novels, daydreaming). I am often aware of my income and the opinions of others. I am affected by rewards and often evaluated. Am I weak? Should I tell the world to bug off, find a rich patron, and settle down to the things I most love to do in the short term? I don't think so. I am afraid that I would lose in the long run. I am afraid that I am normal. The things which give me long-term satisfaction require short-term agony. My values seem to vote against rich patrons. I live in a world of heavy extrinsic motivation. In such a world, rewards are effective and evaluation, inadequate resources, and peer opinion are part of life.

The design of an effective external rewards program for creativity within an organization requires a good bit of sensitivity. As an example, the process should be recognized as well as the product. It is often the case that highly creative developments do not succeed for a reason other than the quality of the work put into the project. Apple's first laptop failed despite the fact that it was consistent with well-done marketing research and technically successful. All indications from the marketing studies were that people wanted the smallest possible computer that would offer all of the characteristics of the desk-top—many hours of battery life, full size keyboard, lots of drives and accessories. The result failed because using the technology of the time resulted in a large and heavy device. At the time no one realized that people would settle for minimal battery life, a smaller keyboard, and the other shortcomings that we accept in order to get a very small package. Apple found that out with its first Powerbook. But the laptop design team was very creative even though the product failed, and the company learned a lot from the attempt. Hopefully the laptop team members were rewarded for their creativity, but in many companies such recognition would be unusual.

It is also necessary to fit the reward to the individual. A reward of $250 might be wonderful to a creative farm worker but insulting to a creative vice president. Publication in a company technical journal might mean more to someone intending an academic career than someone considering technical journals to have little value to the "real world." There are also many forms of reward, all having advantages and disadvantages. Money is a traditional one, but it is controversial. Some people feel it detracts from intrinsic motivation. A classical psychological experiment asked subjects to do a boring repetitive task at different rates of pay. Those receiving higher pay thought the task to be more boring, the apparent reason being that they would not have been paid so much had the task been pleasant. Monetary rewards cost money, so it is cheaper for an organization not to bestow lavish prizes on the more creative. Monetary rewards if given too frequently (the performance bonus) can be assumed to be part of normal pay and therefore lose their effect. Monetary rewards can also complicate life for managers. I once

gave a talk to a company seeking to increase creativity. I later heard from one of its managers that they had returned home from their retreat and tried an experiment.

A particular software design team of eight people was beginning work on a project that the managers assumed would take a year. They asked the team to estimate the earliest date the project could be completed if all went well and if people worked as hard as they could. The answer came back as eight months. This was a project that would result in a large profit if it was finished earlier, so the company offered the team a cash reward of $80,000 ($10,000 per person) if they completed the project in eight months. So far, so good, right? They were one week late! What would you have done as manager of the team? This is one of those situations where there is no good answer. The company gave each member of the group $100. I imagine this makes you groan. However, any solution to the problem would result in some groaning.

These arguments are all valid. The counterargument is that monetary rewards offset the risks involved in creativity and change. There is an increasing amount of experimentation taking place at present. As an example from business, the commission is reemerging in sales. In the past there was a swing toward providing salaries in marketing, not only because it appeared more "professional," but also because sales forces accept corporate goals more easily if they involve selling products that are extremely difficult to move. However, recently people have rediscovered the motivating force of the commission. If you sold one hundred widgets last year and made $50,000 and, if next year I pay you $25,000 and $250 per widget, how many will you sell? The answer is probably more than one hundred. In order to sell more than one hundred you just may become more creative and change your ways.

It is not unusual to offer cash rewards to hourly employees for creative suggestions. In fact, these awards are often a direct function of profit or savings (for example, 10 percent of the net savings over the next year). In the past, it has been unusual to see such awards being given to salaried people, although there is now an increase in monetary rewards to salaried people for creative achievements of the type that would be expected of them anyway.

Indirect uses of monetary reward can also promote creativity and change. In many of these, new activities lead to rapid advancement in a traditional hierarchy, one of the benefits being economic. In one large company that has long had such a system, an employee or a group of employees can present a product concept to a corporate evaluation board. If they find that it has good market potential and is compatible with their business, they will capitalize the development of the concept. If capable, the employee or group supervisor may remain head of the project, which, if successful, will become a division of the company. The project manager will then reap the rewards of a fast organizational climb. This policy was installed because the company has long had a philosophy that at least 25 percent of their sales should be based on products that did not exist five years previously. The policy has worked magnificently. In fact, one of this company's major present worries is its overabundance of divisions, which makes for a rather complex organization chart. Such a reward system, of course, gives the winner much more than money. The psychological rewards associated with promotion and peer esteem are also gained.

## Psychological Rewards

Monetary rewards obviously have a high psychological content. In fact, the psychological component may predominate. Successful founders of companies enjoy their wealth. However, I believe that they enjoy it as a symbol of their creative ability as much as for what it can buy. But rewards can be mainly psychological and escape some of the controversy of monetary awards. Capital flow and salary equity are not concerns and such rewards can be very effective. There are fears about all rewards (they should not be necessary, they will destroy the team, etc.), but I have rarely observed harm caused by well-thought-out psychological rewards. It is true that in certain cases colleagues of a person receiving an individual award will feel more deserving than the recipient. However, there seems to be enough pragmatism/cynicism in all of us to weather that storm and, on the positive side, we realize that someone cares (they just gave the reward to the wrong person). Similarly, in most healthy situations, people are quite pleased when one or a few among them come into possession of something nice. Finally, I have seen few situations where rewards were overdone, especially psychological ones. It is theoretically possible, but most of us are so biased in the other direction that it is not a real worry.

One of the benefits of psychological rewards is that external ones can be internalized. The person who is consistently rewarded for a good chase independently of the kill will come to consider himself or herself a better chaser and, in turn, gain more pleasure from it whether a kill is made or not. The employee who profits from a win in a situation involving creativity and change will be more likely to seek similar situations in the future and be more comfortable in them. People who are well rewarded for creative acts can become self-styled "idea people," obsessed by the need for originality.

Successful psychological rewards for creativity should be applied directly to those doing outstanding work with the maximum possible fanfare. After all, part of their purpose is to emphasize the value that the organization places upon creativity. Individual recognition causes people to be more productive in a creative situation than if they are anonymous in the group. Social psychologists agree with humanistic psychologists that creativity and change are supported by situations in which one can simultaneously be accepted by a group and personally rewarded for the desired activities.

Psychological awards can take many forms. There are the obvious ones like presentations at banquets involving trophies and certificates. Although people, especially highly educated ones, deny their importance and become embarrassed at the presentations, they seem to value them. I have been awarded many such things and I take them home and hide them when my friends visit, but I like them a lot! Publicity is also effective—write-ups, newspapers and magazines, TV spots, displays recognizing employee contributions and such. Managerial compliments are perhaps the cheapest form of psychological feedback for good work and very effective. They are unfortunately rare in certain sectors. Many managers and supervisors simply have difficulty giving compliments. This is partly because in most organizations intellectual interactions take precedence over emotion and partly because either shyness or personal values can get in the way. I am fond of asking groups of managers for a show of hands from those who have decreased their effectiveness by giving out too much praise to those who report to them. I get few hands.

Humor is a useful ingredient in rewards for creativity. Bob McKim, when he was teaching at Stanford, had a particular problem in convincing his students to take risk in one of his senior creativity courses. He therefore inaugurated a prize for the most spectacular failure. Although it had no monetary value, it soon competed in prestige with high grades. Small amounts of money can also result in high positive psychological impact if cleverly spent. I worked with a person once whose contributions were well above the call of duty. We had noticed that he was a lover of single malt scotch. When hosting a party, he would disappear occasionally into the kitchen to dip into his bottle rather than the more mundane brand at the bar. It was obvious that his favorite was a luxury. At one point we had a little party, told him of our gratitude, and gave him a whole case of his favorite single malt. To say he was pleased is an understatement. I think most of us have a secret lust for something that we could probably afford, but which we can't justify buying for ourselves. To have this lust fulfilled as a reward for good work is doubly satisfying.

Professional visibility is an important award. It is a clever organization that recognizes its employees for extraordinary achievement not only within the organization but also outside in the professional field of the particular employee. There is a perceived risk from outside visibility because of the possibility of pirating. However, the risk is more than offset by the reward to the employee. Such visibility is standard procedure in universities, since it is the basis for intellectual communication and advertising. It involves the presentation of papers, publication, and the use of the media. It is an easy perquisite to offer and pays great dividends. Particularly creative research and development groups are masters of this form of reward, which only occasionally can cause problems. I worked at one time for a company, which would send members of its technical staff to any technical meeting that accepted a paper. One person in my division submitted a paper to a conference in Europe, which was duly accepted. Only then did he inform the company that he had a pathological fear of airplanes. Since the policy was so wonderfully open he was able to travel to his conference by train and ship. He had a wonderful time, but was gone for much longer than the company would have liked. As a result there were more provisions added to the policy.

## Support

A few words about support for creativity in organizations are in order, because inadequate support is a major conceptual block. As we mentioned previously, creativity requires resources in the form of people, time, and money. Resources are necessary to accomplish anything worthwhile, even in business as usual. When we talk about change and creativity, we are talking about the allocation of resources in an atmosphere of increased risk and decreased efficiency. As I said in the introduction, I have seen few free lunches through creativity and no major changes accomplished without costs. In fact, the greater the desired creativity and change, the proportionately larger should be the resource investment. This is sometimes a sticking point, because creativity is a word that is often used by people who want more for less.

A small company is successful enough to receive competition from a big one. As the big one tightens the screws, the small company at first assumes that the big company is too traditional and sluggish to harm it and tries to continue on its successful path. At some point things become bad enough, as recognized by shrinking profits, and the company embarks on a frantic effort of increasing creativity. However, by that time, resources are scarce, to say the least. The result is often the demise of the small company. Many examples of this can be seen in the computer business, where small, clever groups of people thought that the H.P.'s of the world just could not move fast enough.

Ambivalence in budgeting may occur because of the long-term nature of creativity and change as opposed to the short-term events of quarterly profits or monthly bills coming due. Even if our problem can be solved by creativity, we may not be able to solve it instantly. We may have to invest real resources in the short term in order to improve our situation in the future. We want a short-term improvement in "more for the buck" and end up with a short-term commitment of "bucks" to get to the desired end. As the short-term wisdom says, R&D comes out of profits (usually this quarter's profits).

For example, when a new computer system is purchased the desired effect, of course, is that efficiency will instantly increase and costs will drop. No way! First of all, employees unfamiliar with the system are pushed into experimentation. They must spend considerable time and effort learning to use the system. Not only must they learn to use it, but they must also become good enough at it so that their performance exceeds that under the old procedures.

Resources must be adequate to cover the experimental nature of a creative venture—the probable wrong turns and unexpected complications. Something new must be taken to a high degree of completion if it is to compete with something old because the world is programmed for business as usual, as is likely the case for influential people within the organization. A business cannot expect a concept on paper to compete with an established product with a sales record. It is difficult to sell the military new concepts in the face of successes in the last war. In order to be bought, concepts must be brought to something close to reality. This requires one-of-a-kind developments which are expensive, time-consuming, and uncertain.

In order to cover contingencies, resources allocated to new directions cannot be simply based on predicted problems, since unpredicted problems are sure to arrive. The only reasonable way to budget for these events is to use past experience in similar new developments. However, even then the uncertainties are such that often the budget can be inadequate both in money and time. This can be seen often in what is called the defense business. Because of the

# Norms for Innovation

| South African Natural Resources Company | European Pharmaceutical Company | U.S. Financial Services Firm | International R&D Managers | Japanese Beer Company |
|---|---|---|---|---|
| Mistakes OK | Rewards | Acceptance of failure | Freedom to fail | Cooperation |
| Recognition | Acceptance of failure | Freedom to try things | Risk taking | Mistakes OK |
| Rewards | —careful | —time | —fast | Openness |
| Mutual respect | —learn | —support | —prudent | Flexibility |
| Open communication | —calculated | —resources | —cheap | Clear direction |
| Freedom to experiment | Clear objectives | Clear goals | Rewards | Ideas are valued |
| Expectation of change | Sharing of information | Celebration of success | Involvement | Rewards for innovation |
| Challenge the status quo | Teamwork | Removal of barriers to change | Toleration of dissent | |
| Equal partners | Commitment from the top | Setting an example | Listening | |
| | Empowerment | Resources | Positive role models | |
| | | | Resources | |

From *Winning Through Innovation* M. Tushman, C. O'Reilly, Harvard Business School Press, Boston, Mass., 1997 advantage of technological superiority and the complexity of modern warfare, the military is extraordinarily good at asking for products that are unprecedented. Because of the way in which contracts are awarded, technical optimism, and past successes, companies will bid aggressively for the work. Schedules then slip and costs overrun and we are all familiar with the media coverage that results. The creativity and change involved in this work are great. Our ability to predict resource needs and schedule is less. Is it incompetence and dishonesty that results in so many examples of budgets being exceeded and schedules being missed, or is some of it perhaps due to a lack of appreciation for the unknowns involved? I heard the CEO of a large provider of sophisticated weapons to the Department of Defense give a talk shortly after the company had taken a fierce drubbing for exceeding their budget and missing their schedule. He commented that never in history had any agency been as good at asking for the impossible as the Department of Defense and never in history were there so many suckers like his company ready to submit a low bid for the privilege of providing it.

## Culture

In their book *Winning through Innovation* Tushman and O'Reilly laud the importance of the proper organizational culture to innovation. In their discussion, they describe the culture of five unusually creative and very different companies. A brief summary is shown in the previous figure. No surprises there for those of us who study creativity, and organizations who have cultures such as these should not only feel fortunate but worry a lot about maintaining them. But many organizations who wish to be more creative are far from these models. How do they change their cultures to be more consistent with their wish? Tushman and O'Reilly prescribe several tools to shape the culture of an organization. One is rigorous selection. Organizations who wish to change should ensure that the process that brings in new people changes. I have had a great deal of experience with company representatives hiring college graduates, and their criteria do not always match the desires of the top management of the company. Company management may be devoutly seeking new directions and more innovation and the recruiters may be looking for docile gofers. This is particularly likely in large companies where the rank-and-file may not especially desire the necessary change.

"I know that buggies are becoming obsolete, but I can find more uses for buggy whips if I can just hire enough good buggy whip people to help me." To change a culture it is necessary to bring in people compatible with the new directions who are strong enough to withstand the influence of the old.

Another tool Tushman and O'Reilly mention is socialization—efforts to ensure that new employees, and for that matter old ones, are exposed to the core values of the desired culture. A good example of a very successful socialization process is the basic training of the U.S. Marine Corps. They also suggest shaping organizational cultures through participation and commitment. If we are actively involved in an activity, we become committed to its importance. One of my favorite psychological theories is that of cognitive dissonance. It says that we do not like dissonance in our minds, so we resolve conflicts, but in a way which makes us seem like we have the right answer. It is interesting to watch college-bound high-school seniors anguish over which college to apply to. After two weeks on the campus of the one they attend, they can hardly believe they considered any other. It is an interesting fact that people read new-car literature more thoroughly after they buy the car— reinforcement that they made a brilliant choice. If we are putting our all into creative work, it would be hard to think that we are wasting our time. Much better to think that it is the most important type of work around.

The use of rewards and recognition is yet another tool they recommend. We talked about both of these in the previous section. My university is heavily devoted to research and believes that through this research we can keep classroom material both current and exciting. However, in order to remain strong in research it is necessary to hire faculty members who love to do research and supervise Ph.D. students and to raise large amounts of money. Over the past years our culture has become strongly biased toward these activities and we are now in an effort to strengthen the undergraduate program. The university is successfully using both rewards and recognition to do this, although we are definitely not considering doing it at the expense of the research program. If we were, we would have a much harder time of it. It is easier to add something to a culture than to subtract.

Finally, Tushman and O'Reilly also prescribe the use of symbolic management acts. This is a particularly powerful tool and has great influence on an organization. At one time in Hewlett Packard's history, when quality improvement was in the wind, the company set an extraordinarily ambitious goal. They succeeded partly because John Young, the CEO, made it his #1 goal and made sure that everyone knew it. Don Petersen did the same when he was President of Ford Motor Company. Bob Galvin the past president of Motorola, was personally extremely interested in creativity. His interest was widely enough known and often enough expressed by him that it had a very positive effect on the already high creativity level in the company. Ideally such symbolic acts should take place at all levels of management. I have had personal experience reporting to a strong manager who did not agree with necessary changes that were happening in the company culture. I can report that it left me and some of my friends who also reported to him in somewhat of a tight spot.

As a final comment, changing an organizational culture is a creative act and requires confronting conceptual blocks. As we have seen, these blocks inhibit creativity, but they also simplify life. It is exciting to overcome them, but like any change, effort is required and uncertainty may result. If I am a manager and the people who report to me are competent, and therefore have alternate possible ways to spend their time, they are not going to change simply because I tell them to. Changing a culture requires sensitivity to the individuals and groups in that culture and the ability to convince them that their lives will be better for the change. I have been involved in many attempts to change organizational cultures and it is difficult indeed. However, thinking about the specific and common conceptual blocks in this book helps me in the process. Should you be in a similar spot, I hope you will find the book useful.

# Reader's Guide

IN THE ORIGINAL EDITION of this book, published in 1974, I described a number of books about creativity that I thought were interesting and helpful. I suggested books since they were generally more available than papers. Most of them in turn contained bibliographies of books, papers, and other materials, allowing the interested reader to work my few suggestions into an extensive list, should she/he desire. At that time I was familiar with most of the literature and felt comfortable in making suggestions. I am going to suggest some books to read again, but I must warn you that times have changed. Bookstores now contain much larger numbers of books on the subjects and libraries are awash with material. As of the time of this writing there are almost 1800 books listed under the heading of creativity on Amazon.com's web site (1388 in print on the Barnes and Noble site, with vast numbers out of print). The numbers under innovation and imagination are larger. One search engine happily offers me 1,350,000 matches to the word creativity. Please don't think less of me if I tell you I have not read all of this material.

This explosion in the written material concerning creativity has happened in the past 25 years. This despite the fact that there is no complete and scientifically verified explanation of creative thinking. Still, in this mountain of reading, one finds a large number of hypotheses, ranging from simplistic to elegant, which shed light on the creative act. There are innumerable techniques for increasing individual, group, and organizational creativity, most of which work for someone and few which work for everyone. Finally there are thoughtful (and nonthoughtful) treatises on what creativity means for all of us.

This material contains a large amount of conjecture and many value judgements which the reader must sort through and accept or discard depending on whether he/she is convinced or not (or probably on whether or not the reader's own opinions and values are reinforced). However, I suggest you attack the pile. As computers have helped make the pile larger, so have they made it somewhat easier to sort. When encountering theories be suspicious of any claims of complete understanding. In the case of creativity "techniques," look for those that "fit" you and be suspicious of any that promise instant genius or unlimited wealth without any work on your part.

I am going to give you the names of some books I particularly like, but be forewarned that my opinion is anything but "the final word." I have often gotten myself into trouble by assigning readings to a class and telling them to skip certain portions because they are of less value. Invariably one (or several) of the students will read these portions (presumably to see why they are of less value) and tell me that they are the most important parts of the reading. I also have gotten into trouble from not recommending books that people I know love (or write). Therefore, take my comments with a grain of salt and spend your effort reading what seems to be of most value to you.

## General Overviews of Creativity

*Creativity and Beyond* is an ambitious book on the nature of creativity by Robert Paul Weiner (New York: State University of New York Press, 2000). The author has a broad background in the humanities and treats the topic of creativity from viewpoints ranging from the historical to the contemporary. This book is of particular interest to those seriously interested in the topic of creativity. An older but classic book that has been widely quoted is *The Act of Creation*, by Arthur Koestler (New York: Penguin, 1990). George F. Kneller, who was active in the study of creativity at the time it was written, called it "the most ambitious attempt yet made to integrate the findings of a range of disciplines into a single theory of creativity. In this book, bold in its ideas and profusely documented, Koestler seeks to synthesize his own theory of the nature of creativity, as manifested in humor, art, and science, with the latest conclusions of psychology, physiology, neurology, genetics, and a number of other sciences" How about that!

There was a relatively large amount of writing on creativity in the 1960's, perhaps in part catalyzed by unhappiness over the conventionality of the 1950's. If you would like a look at the type of thinking that was occurring at the time, try to find a now out-of-print book entitled *A Source Book for Creative Thinking*, edited by Sidney J. Parnes and Harold F. Harding. It was originally published by Scribners and Sons in 1962. It contained a collection of 29 articles and 75 research summaries by people such as Abraham Maslow, Carl Rogers, Alex Osborne, John

Arnold, Frank Barron, and other luminaries of creativity studies of the time, as well as a bibliographical discussion of material then available.

A number of books treat creativity by focusing on individuals who are/were considered to be unusually creative. Two venerable ones are *The Creative Process*, edited by Brewster Ghiselin (Berkeley: University of California Press, 1996) and *The Mathematician's Mind*, by Jacques Hadamard (Princeton, NJ: Princeton University Press, 1996). The first is a series of writings by famous writers, visual artists, and scientists (Mozart, Einstein, Poincare, etc.) that speak to the creative process as seen by the authors. They cover many phenomena, such as Mozart's alleged ability to hear music, and then simply write it down, that are folklore among those who write about creativity. The second is a study of creativity among outstanding mathematicians and scientists. It is an attempt by the author, himself a well-known mathematician, to explain mathematical and scientific invention.

Many more books by and about highly creative people allow the reader to muse upon the creative process. One of my long-time favorites is *The Double Helix*, by James Watson. This is the author's story of the discovery of the structure of DNA which subsequently resulted in the Nobel prize for him and his collaborators Francis Crick and Maurice Wilkins. It is a story so contradictory to some stereotypes of science that a well-known academic publishing house refused to publish it. The gory details of this controversy are contained in a version edited by Gunther Stent (New York: W. W. Norton, 1981). Three other good stories are *The Life and Science of Richard Feynman* by James Gleik (New York: Pantheon, 1992), *The Starship and the Canoe*, by Kenneth Brower (New York: HarperCollins, 1983), and *Soul of a New Machine*, by Tracy Kidder (Boston: Little Brown & Co., 2000). The physicist Richard Feynman has drawn a large amount of attention not only because of his brilliance in his field but also the colorfulness of his character. *The Starship and the Canoe* is an entertaining double-biography of Freeman Dyson, also an eminent physicist, and his son George. Freeman was at one point part of Project Orion, a group that was attempting to harness nuclear energy to drive huge spacecraft capable of reaching other star systems. George's very different values led him to a life in a tree house in British Columbia and of striving after the perfect kayak. I have frequently used this book in my classes and asked the students to compare the two. They are both extremely creative, in many ways similar, and in others very different. *Soul of a New Machine*, although now a bit dated, is the best story I know about a high-technology development in a company. It gives the reader plenty to think about as far as creativity in a corporation is concerned.

For an outstanding treatment of the subject of genius, read *Origins of Genius*, by Dean Keith Simonton (New York: Oxford, 1999). This book covers a large amount of research on highly creative people and the author's original thinking on the roots of genius and the nature of creativity. It is beautifully written and extremely thought provoking. This is an extremely interesting topic to me, because I know quite a few people who may merit the "genius" label, but they seem to me to be disturbingly normal. I have yet to meet anyone like the Mozart portrayal in the movie *Amadeus*.

## Thinking

Many books on the general topic of thinking either directly or indirectly treat creativity. One of my favorites is *Mindfulness*, by Ellen J. Langer (Cambridge: Perseus Publishing, 1989). It treats the habitual nature of thinking, and is filled with entertaining examples and exercises. It could have as well been titled "Mindlessness." Over the years there have been many books and individuals questioning the simplistic measure of the I.Q. test and proposing different measures of intelligence. They tend to make one think about thinking. One of the pioneers in this area was J. P. Guilford. Two of his books, *Intelligence, Creativity, and their Educational Implications* and *Creative Talents, their Nature, Uses, and Development*, are still available and give an good indication of his thinking. A widely read book on so-called multiple intelligences is *Frames of Mind*, by Howard Gardner (New York: Basic Books, 1985). This book and Gardner's work have had considerable impact in educational circles, as they emphasize the loss of opportunity from looking too narrowly at the meaning of intelligence.

As you can tell from reading this book, I find the topic of cognitive style of great interest. Perhaps the most popular instrument for attempting to define it is the Myers-Briggs Type Inventory, based on the theory of Carl Jung. It is available from the Consulting Psychologists Press, Palo Alto, California, but only to qualified professionals. A book offering a contemporary approach to this type of characterization is *Please Understand Me II*, by David Kiersey, (Del Mar: Prometheus Nemesis, 1998). Another extremely well-done treatment of the application of Jungian theory to creativity is *Breakthrough Creativity*, by Lynne Levesque, Palo Alto, Davies-Black, 2001)

Finally, since memory is so central to problem solving, a couple of books on memory are in order. You might be interested in *Don't Forget*, by Danielle C. Lapp (Reading: Addison-Wesley, 1995) and *Memory*, by Larry R. Squire and Eric R. Kandel (New York: W. H. Freeman, 2000). The first is a general discussion of memory including exercises for the purpose of improving one's memory. The second discusses the mechanics of memory as understood by those working in the neurosciences. The first is a much easier read than the second, but for those of a scientific bent of mind, *Memory* is a good book for an update on how neuroscientists view memory.

## Psychological Theory

Since much creativity theory is directly drawn from psychology, the psychological literature is of great interest. If you have never taken an introductory psychology course (Psych 1) you should read a good general introductory book to psychology in order to learn the words, the concepts, the names, and the fundamental theories. Two good ones are Hilgard's *Introduction to Psychology*, by Rita L. Atkinson, et al. (New York: Harcourt, 2000) and *Basic Psychology*, by Henry Gleitman (New York: W. W. Norton, 1999).

Two books by contemporary psychologists that are well worth reading are *Creativity in Context*, by Teresa M. Amabile (Boulder: Westview Press, 1996) and *Creativity*, by Mihaly Csikszentmihalyi (New York: HarperCollins, 1996). In my opinion, Amabile is one of the best researchers in the area of creativity and is particularly concerned with reward. Her book makes a case for the importance of intrinsic reward. The Csikszentmihalyi book includes interviews with large numbers of highly creative people and hypothesizes a characteristic he calls flow as being central to creativity.

If you would like to delve into the theories of Freud and Jung, I suggest *On Creativity and the Unconscious*, by Sigmund Freud (New York: Harper, 1958), and *Man And His Symbols*, edited by Carl Jung (New York: Dell Publishing Co., 1970). The first is a collection of writings by Freud that are concerned with cultural and humanist matters. Many of the selections in the book deal with the particular problems of creative people and reflections upon psychoanalysis and are therefore only marginally pertinent to conceptualization. However, part of the book does treat conceptualization specifically and the book is an interesting insight into some of the lesser known interests of Freud. *Man And His Symbols* is a translation of Jungian psychology into language accessible to the lay reader. It was put together by Jung and several collaborators during the last years of Jung's life.

## The Mind/Brain and the Senses

A few years ago, the media was fond of referring to the "cognitive" revolution. This referred to the rapidly increasing understanding of the brain and nervous system due to the impetus from the information business, interesting metaphors from computer science, more sophisticated instrumentation, and improved bio-chemical knowledge. An outpouring of literature has accompanied this. Although an increased knowledge of the brain (the machine) and mind (the machine in action) may not directly affect one's creativity, it is certainly helpful in understanding the process and its limitations. As a good introductory book on the brain, I suggest *The Brain*, by Richard F. Thompson (New York: W. H. Freeman, 2000). This is a book that is intended to be used in introductory psychology classes, so it is readable without a neuroscience background and filled with interesting material.

An older book of interest is *Maps Of The Mind*, by C. Hampden Turner (New York: Collier Books, 1982). It briefly reviews a large number of models of the mind that have withstood the test of time, briefly describing, explaining, and commenting on the importance of each. Finally, one of my favorite books is *A Natural History of the Senses*, by Diane Ackerman (New York: Vintage, 1991). This is a beautifully written book that makes heavy use of metaphor to discuss the senses. I use it often in classes because it not only gives one a greater understanding of the senses, but at least temporarily causes the reader to be more aware of sensory information.

## Creativity in Business

Much of the impetus for the attention paid to creativity during the past 20 years has been the high interest in innovation on the part of business. This interest has resulted in a large market for books, since business people have a large appetite for knowledge that can improve their lot (and of course, companies often pay for the books). This knowledge alone, of course, does not guarantee business success. The reader interested in creativity in business might begin by reading *The Knowing-Doing Gap*, by Jeffrey Pfeffer and Robert I. Sutton (Boston: Harvard Business School Press, 2000) which attempts to explain why so many managers in business fail to apply what they know. Three other books that should appeal to those seeking to increase innovation in organizations are *Winning Through Innovation*, by Michael Tushman, and Charles A. O'Reilly III (Boston: Harvard Business School Press, 1997),

*The Innovator's Dilemma*, by Clayton M. Christensen (Boston: Harvard Business School Press, 1997), and *Weird Ideas That Work*, by Robert I Sutton (New York: Free Press, N.Y., 2001). The first is a general book on the management of innovation in an organization and the second focuses on large successful companies that are damaged by what the author terms "disruptive" technologies. The third is also focused on innovation in general, but is particularly interesting because it is structured upon a number of concepts that are counter to traditional business traditions. All three of these books contain ample bibliographies.

*Stream Analysis*, by Jerry Porras (Reading: Addison-Wesley, 1987) was mentioned earlier in the text. It is concerned with problem definition—how does one isolate "core" problems rather than spending time on symptoms. The books on Japanese business that abounded in the 1980s are still worth reading because the Japanese were and are terribly successful at process creativity. Although we in the U.S. have learned a great deal, we still sometimes become obsessed with invention and overlook the creativity needed to implement well. A good example of such a book is *Made In Japan*, written by Akio Morita, the founder of Sony (New York: E. P. Dutton, 1986).

Another interesting book on creativity in business is *Jamming*, by John Kao, (New York: HarperCollins, 1996). In this book Kao relies on a jazz metaphor (jamming) to discuss some of the problems confronting innovation in a company and some techniques to overcome them. On the issue of the creative team. I highly recommend *The Wisdom of Teams*, by Jon R. Katzenbach and Douglas K. Smith (Boston: Harvard Business School Press, 1993). This book outlines the principle characteristics of highly effective teams and discusses how one gets there. Although the book is not directly about creativity, it is now generally conceded that much creativity is the result of group work, rather than the statement of an individual.

In this book I have talked about the inhibition of creativity that can result from the actions of overly dominant individuals. However, influence and power are part and parcel of life and creative people need to be able to exert the necessary influence to see their ideas become reality. Also a better understanding of influence and power arms one to deal with it better if it is being used to block one's efforts. In this regard I recommend two excellent books. The first is *Influence*, by Robert Cialdini, (New York, Harper Collins, 1993), a wonderful read that describes a number of commonly used and highly effective approaches to influencing other people. It will not only educate and entertain you, but make you realize how you are being manipulated by skillful people. The other is *Managing with Power,* by Jeffrey Pfeffer (Boston, Harvard Business School Press, 1992). In it, Pfeffer talks about all aspects of organizational power from what it is and how to gain and use it to how it is lost.

## "How to" books

There is a large demand for books containing techniques and tools oriented toward increasing creativity and the result can be overwhelming. When I first became interested in creativity, there were many fewer, and in my initial excitement I set forth to learn as many of these tools and techniques as I could. Unfortunately I discovered that the mind does not have a pull-down menu, allowing one to periodically select the optimal technique from one's palette. I find I am better off with a small number that best augment the natural fumbling of my mind. That is why I attempted to categorize them in this book. I recommend that you be discriminating in your search. Many are attractive because they are fun, interesting, and challenging, but make sure they are useful to you, unless you merely want to be entertained by reading about them.

Two books typical of the genre are *Thinkertoys,* by Michael Michalko (Berkeley: Ten Speed Press, 1991) and *101 Creative Problem Solving Techniques,* by James M. Higgins (Winter Park, FL: The New Management Publishing Company, 1994). Although both are oriented toward business, they contain a large number of tricks and approaches that could be used in a number of situations. Other examples are *The Universal Traveler,* by Don Koberg and Jim Bagnall (Los Altos, CA: William Kaufmann Inc., 1980), *Wake Up Your Creative Genius,* by Kurt Hanks and Jay A. Parry (Los Altos, CA: William Kaufmann, 1983), and *Lateral Thinking,* by Edward De Bono (New York: Harper and Row, 1990), a very prolific writer on the subject of creativity.

Some of these books emphasize routines to alter one's problem-solving style. The *Mind Map Book,* by Tony Buzan and Barry Buzan (New York: Dutton, 1996) proposes graphically portraying the thinking process in order to derive creative solutions. *A Whack on the Side of the Head,* by Roger Von Oech (New York: Time-Warner Books, 1998), proposes a number of methods of stirring up the thinking process. One of the most widely used creativity techniques is brainstorming, originally described by Alex Osborn in his book *Applied Imagination* (New York: Scribner, 1957). Brainstorming has become part of the contemporary vocabulary, but some of you might like to see what Osborne, who is credited with the approach, had to say about it.

A large number of other "how to" books can be found by visiting any large library, bookstore, or your friendly world wide web. Browse away!

## Miscellaneous

As stated in the book, emotional blocks are an important inhibition to creativity. A popular book treating this topic is *Emotional Intelligence*, by Daniel Goleman (New York: Bantam, 1997). In the first part of this book, the author reviews the research on emotion, and in the last he suggests methods that might cause our emotions to be more in line with accomplishing our goals. Douglas Hofstadter has written three books that stretch the mind. These are *Godel, Escher, and Bach* (New York: Basic Books, 1999), *The Mind's I* (New York: Basic Books, 2001), and *Metamagical Themas* (New York: Basic Books, 1996). The first is a somewhat esoteric investigation of similarities between the work of Godel, Escher, and Bach. The second is an investigation of self, and very pertinent to those who think about thinking. One cannot go very far in this pastime without coming across the elusiveness of the concept "I." The third is based upon a column that Hofstadter wrote for Scientific American. It is full of brain-stretchers, puzzles, and enigmas.

Speaking of puzzles, if you like such things look in the mathematical section of your library. Mathematicians have a soft spot for such pastimes. There is even a *Journal of Recreational Mathematics*, put out by the Baywood Publishing Company. Most puzzle and game books cater to a wide range of mathematical prowess. Examples are those written and collected by Martin Gardner, who was for many years the puzzle editor of *Scientific American Magazine*. Examples are *Aha! Insight* (New York: W. H. Freeman, 1978), *Aha! Gotcha* (New York: W. H. Freeman, 1982), *My Best Mathematical and Logic Puzzles* (New York: Dover, 1994). *Perplexing Puzzles and Tantalizing Teasers* (New York: Dover, 1988) and *Hexaflexagons and other Mathematical Diversions* (Chicago: University of Chicago Press, 1988). Even if you are uncomfortable about mathematics, you should find material in such books that will keep you off the street for a while.

# Index